MY BORO DEBUT

Published in paperback in 2020 by Sixth Element Publishing
on behalf of Robert Nichols

Sixth Element Publishing
Arthur Robinson House
13-14 The Green
Billingham TS23 1EU
Tel: 01642 360253
www.6epublishing.net

ISBN 978-1-912218-98-1

British Library Cataloguing in Publication Data. A catalogue record
for this book is available from the British Library.

Printed in Great Britain.

Cover Photo by Paul Thompson
westyorkshireimages.photoshelter.com

MY BORO DEBUT

EDITED BY
ROBERT NICHOLS

INTRODUCTION

I don't remember my Boro debut but I remember my brother's...

Maybe that isn't the best way to introduce a book documenting Boro fans' first games but fortunately there are an awful lot of people out there with a far better memory than me. Memories that demonstrate that those first faltering steps inside the Boro ground are right up there with the most important days in fans' lives.

We all have first games, don't we, and even if some people share a match, the experience is going to be unique. The emotional umbilical chord is forged at debut and it stays with you.

I had been mulling over this book for a long time. Then when lockdown hit home in March 2020 with the bang of the bolted front door, well, that really fixed my mind. How to escape the four walls? How to reach out to others similarly confined?

Then I got to thinking that the simple action of going to the match that we have all taken for granted for so long was no longer a given. A real game changer. Our Middlesbrough memories are what we have left and they suddenly seem even more precious. It was more important than ever to make a record of Boro fans' first footing along their long and winding road of fandom.

After nearly half a century of my own Boro worship, I seem to have amassed a really big group of Boro fan friends and contacts and it was to them I turned via email, twitter and facebook messenger. I didn't want to disturb anyone on the phone at what might have been a very challenging time. This meant that in true fanzine fashion, this book is made up of accounts by the fans, for the fans. It is well over 150 fan voices set down on computer keyboards or mobiles. So, very much in the fans' own words. Accounts often written from the heart. Fans and ex-players all in this together. Also, we have a good few more high profile fans from darts champions to commentators to writers and to music stars. They all belong to the Boro family. Through this book, we trace generations passing on the Boro baton down the line. Rites of passage perhaps taken on the trackless or O bus or more recently through the underpass to the Riverside.

Look around you when you finally return to the match. These personal accounts are penned by fans sitting in the four stands. They are for the most part home and away supporters, with years and years of suffering and elation between them. This is personal, yes, but also community. That makes this little book a very special collection of Boro fan memories, relating the day where and when it all began for them, the trigger point, where perhaps a parent took their child and nothing was ever the same again.

Oh, back to my brother Stephen's first match: Boro 4 – 1 York City in the FA Cup 1970. He was five years old. His son, my six-year-old nephew Sam, travelled 6,000 miles from Hong Kong to watch Gareth Southgate's Boro lose 3-0 at Craven Cottage on December 20th 2008. He was straight off the plane and into a defeat. Six days later, Boxing Day and his

Riverside debut and a 0-1 defeat to Everton. "The Boro are getting worse," was his post game verdict but it didn't ruin his Christmas and he remains a long distance fan all these years later.

Boro does seem to run through our blood and in this book fans listed in first name alphabetical order give their own Boro stories. Yet we must start and end with one family tree, that leads right through from the 1940s to the 2000s…

To all the generations that passed before and all Boro debuts to come, and looking forward to full houses at the Riverside again.

Come On Boro and Up The Boro

Robert Nichols

Fly Me To The Moon fanzine

www.fmttm.com

These memories may sometimes differ from the record books but they are 100% from the heart.

MY FIRST BORO MATCH
AYRESOME PARK, 1946/47
JACK BOLTON

My first Boro game is a bit of a blur in terms of the match itself but it came at the start of the 1946/47 season that was special not just for me but millions of others as The Football League resumed after the end of World War II following a seven-season break.

The excitement was tangible as I walked from home with my dad to the match. There were no floodlights in those days to see Ayresome Park from afar but with over 40,000 expected at home matches by the time we reached Albert Park, the Boro fans had grown significantly in number and they were all heading for the same destination.

Approaching the stadium, I remember seeing scores of supporters' bicycles lined up outside front doors, the owners having paid the householders for the privilege!

On entering the stadium, we went behind the goal (the Bob End). At the back of the stand there were metal plates where at half-time, scores from other matches were displayed.

I recall there was a brass band on the pitch before the match. An old man walked around the edge of the pitch, pushing a wooden barrow that had two big wheels. It held a large blackboard with team changes (from the match programme team list) chalked on it.

That day I witnessed some all-time great players, such as Micky Fenton, George Hardwick and Wilf Mannion, don the famous red shirt of Middlesbrough Football Club.

That first match experience was the start of a life-long love affair with Boro and 74 years later I still feel that tangible excitement when I go to the match.

BORO 5 – 3 LEEDS UNITED
AYRESOME PARK, DECEMBER 24TH 1955
ALAN EBBS

I was seven years old and staying with grandparents for Christmas in Pym Street, South Bank (now sadly demolished). Dad (who was a Luton fan) and I left by trackless from Bennett's Corner to North Ormesby and cut through the passage by the abattoir, to meet up with an uncle and cousin living in Muriel Street near the Maternity Hospital, by Albert Park.

We then went into Ayresome Park and stood near the corner flag on the Clive Road side, where the away fans gathered in later days.

As many have mentioned before, the sight of the green expanse before us under the floodlights was something to behold. A lasting first memory. I had been to several grounds before but this was captivating!

Now to the match. Charlie Wayman returned as centre forward, replacing a certain B. Clough. The initial memory of the match was this dusky spectre speeding down the wing. It was Lindy Delapenha and he gained a corner in the opening minutes. The match was evenly balanced, with the legendary John Charles being dangerous for them.

Then two quick goals came for Boro, Wayman on 6 minutes. A minute later Delapenha scored. Charles was still causing Boro problems and Leeds pulled back with two goals, Hutchinson on 38 minutes and Charles 3 minutes later. Boro had the last laugh of the first half though with Wayman scoring on 44 minutes. Leeds pulled back again on 52 minutes with a goal from Vickers. The game continued to be even until late on when Delapenha scored with a 35 yarder on 78 minutes and Scott made the game safe on 83 minutes.

The Leeds centre half that day was a certain Jack Charlton. I wonder what became of him?

NIL-NIL ON A GREY DAY
AYRESOME PARK, 1968/69
ALAN MORLEY, ARTIST

Boro had been relegated to the Third Division in the mid-1960s and won promotion back to Division Two for the start of the '67 season. I'm sure it was the 1968/69 season though that dad took me to one of the games after I had caught him out several times sneaking to Ayresome Park on a Saturday.

I'm a Linthorpe boy and like many around the old ground could hear in the street when Boro scored and hear the Holgate even when it was in full song, and we were streets away; we lived near the Palladium shops. My distinct memory was playing in the street and seeing dad in his army issue khaki coat (which young folk won't realise was fashionable even before we tend to remember Army and Navy Store stuff being the rage in the long-haired '70s). I would ask him where he was going and he would always say, "See a man about a dog."

Anyway, in the end, he caved in and paid for a seat for me next to him in the East End Seats; he traditionally stood in the South Stand Terrace opposite the Clock Stand before going for a jar with buddies, perhaps in the Village. On this day it was classically British with cloud cover and was completely grey. Everything seemed to be psychologically grey apart from the opposing team who were in light blue.

Being a primary school kid fresh out of the infants, I haven't a clue who we were playing. I was consumed with the sights, smells and atmosphere of this strange world and didn't really follow what was going on. Dad was hoping for his favourites John O'Rourke or Hickton to come on as subs – so there's a good clue for a geek to narrow down – they must've been recovering from injuries. Dad wanted a goal so I could experience the celebration of my first one like a father wanting his son to lose his cherry to a good girl. It didn't happen and my grey day was a bit long and a bit 'Boro flat'. 'Nil-nil' became part of my vocabulary but boy were things about to change. Four years later I had matured somewhat and Jackie Charlton landed. A return to the East End Seats for the full season was to be in technicolour!

BORO 0 – 1 HUDDERSFIELD TOWN
AYRESOME PARK, DECEMBER 26TH 1957
ALAN SPENCE

Our dad was a life-long Sunderland supporter and we even had a cousin (also called Alan Spence) who played a few games for the Makems, before journeying his way round several clubs as a semi-pro footballer/PE teacher.

In spite of all this, my first game at the Boro was Middlesbrough v Huddersfield Town December 26th 1957. I was nine years old. My brother, who took me, was twelve. Despite it being Boxing Day, the weather was mild, and after a United 72 from South Bank and the walk from the bus station, we arrived at Ayresome Park.

I can't remember going through the turnstiles, but going up the stairs and onto the Boys End, I noticed it was sparsely attended. The kind of self-distancing that has become so familiar recently. One other issue, if I moved towards the front wall, I could hardly see anything and had to position myself several steps back.

The pitch seemed to stretch into the distance and the weather had taken a turn for the worse, with fog covering much of the far end of the pitch and the Holgate End. When the teams came out, Huddersfield attacked the Boys End to no avail, but with the increasing fog we saw little of the Boro action at the Holgate End. The scores were level.

The second half got no better, Boro tried, but never looked like scoring, that was action we could have been spared, at least Huddersfield hadn't either. At least we had got a draw or so we thought. When we got home, BBC Sports Report said Huddersfield had won 0-1. How our dad laughed. Great!!

Result: Middlesbrough 0 Huddersfield Town 1.
(Ledger) Att 22,964.

A final historical note: the 57/58 season was Bill Shankly's first in charge of Huddersfield and one Dennis Law played for The Terriers.

BORO 2 – 1 FC SEATTLE STORM
AYRESOME PARK, FRIENDLY, JULY 20TH 1987
DR ALEX GILLETT, PHD

My first Boro game was on 20th July1987, a friendly game against FC Seattle Storm, held at Ayresome Park. I was there with my dad and my grandad (who had been part of the Boro team from 1946 to 1950, although due to injury his involvement was limited to playing in the Reserve team). Possibly my Uncle Andy too. Although all Boro fans, we were there as guests of Seattle, as my dad's cousin Dave Gillett was on the staff and had played for the Seattle Sounders (the team which existed before the Storm). The connection was Bruce Rioch, who was at that time the manager of Middlesbrough, but had previously played for the Sounders.

We got to sit in the Away team's Directors' Box. I remember having a drink in one of the bars before the game (just a cola for me, I was nine years old). Things get a bit hazy after that because I also went to the rematch when Seattle returned to Ayresome in 1988, for my second game, and memories begin to mix up. At one of the games, before the main event there was an exhibition match – I'm not entirely sure who played in it but technically that could have been the first game I saw.

In 1987 (2-1 to the Boro) I think we must have gone straight home afterwards, but in 1988 (3-0 Boro win) I remember quite clearly that we stayed on in one of the bars inside the North Stand, where we met up with Dave and the Seattle team and staff. The Boro squad were also all in there and I got most, if not all of the players and staff from both teams to autograph my programme, a souvenir 'Stormin The Isles Tour of Britain' brochure produced by Seattle. I was a bit shy because these were 'football stars' but everyone was friendly and happy to sign an autograph. At the time I remember thinking how tall Gary Pallister was, although now I'm grown up I'm around the same height.

The first 'competitive' game that I went to was v Spurs in January 1989. My dad and I stood in the Holgate, near the top and towards the corner near the South Stand. A 2-2 draw, and an eventful game. Boro fans threw Mars Bars at Paul Gascoigne, a joke about his physique, and although he seemed to find it funny at first, either the joke wore thin or someone shouted something he didn't enjoy hearing, because he got a bit wound-up at one point. Most memorable though was a great long-range goal, I think by Colin Cooper, which seemed to come out of nowhere.

BORO 1 – 3 SWANSEA
AYRESOME PARK, FEBRUARY 10TH 1962
ALEX WILSON

I went to my first ever Boro match aged nine, a home game against Swansea Town on February 10th 1962. The attendance was 11,220. We were robbed and I'm not talking about on the pitch. Abject doesn't come into it. Beaten 1-3 to send us to the bottom of the second division. I can still remember Cliff Mitchell's headline in the Gazette : 'Boro Hit Rock Bottom'. It shouldn't have been like that. The Boro team that day was Bob Appleby, Gordon Jones, Mick McNeil, Derek Stonehouse, the tragic Ken Thomson, Ray Yeoman, Eddie Holliday in his last game of this spell for Boro, Billy Day, Arthur Kaye, Joe Livingstone and Bill Harris. Mick McNeil and Eddie Holliday were both full England internationals and Gordon Jones was under-23 captain. Bill Harris had a couple of caps for Wales. Alan Peacock was injured for a change. I don't remember much about the game itself other than the fact Swansea played in all white, went 3-0 up and by the time Livingstone scored, half the crowd had gone. It was crap. Next game for me was Sunderland. They won 1-0 (Clough) and Peacock got his jaw broken after 10 seconds.

BORO 3 – 1 SHEFFIELD WEDNESDAY
RIVERSIDE STADIUM, APRIL 5TH 1996
ANDY CAMPBELL, FORMER BORO PLAYER

My debut against Sheffield Wednesday was amazing but very surreal. Seeing the stadium full and knowing all my friends and family there made is so much more special. Waiting to come on felt like an age and the gaffer just said, "Go and enjoy it." I loved every second of it. I was nervous before and during but they went when I got on and I tried to impress everyone. Pulling on that red shirt meant so much to me. Probably the best moment in football. Being a fan and then living the dream to play for my home town club. I looked up to all the players when I started playing. The older players, including Robbie Mustoe, Steve Vickers, Curtis Fleming, all helped me each day in training and to settle in. My first real memories of watching as a fan were the Bradford City play off game. I think we won 2-1 in the second leg. Also the ZDS win over Villa and then the 1-0 defeat at Wembley v Chelsea. I'll never forgive Tony Dorigo. He broke my heart that day but it was a great experience to go and watch my team with my family.

BORO 8 – 0 SHEFFIELD WEDNESDAY
AYRESOME PARK, SATURDAY 20TH APRIL 1974
ANDY CARR

My grandparents lived next door but one to the Holgate End, number 3 Addison Road to be exact.

I used to watch the crowds build up ahead of the matches from the front room window. I'd kneel on the chair and look out in sheer amazement at how many people were gathering and waiting to head into the ground.

On Saturday 20th April 1974, at the age of six years old, I finally got a chance to join them for the first time in Ayresome Park as I accompanied my grandfather to watch Charlton's Champions hammer Sheffield Wednesday by eight to nil. I remember very little about the game but that is when my love affair with Middlesbrough Football Club started and all these years later I can still recite the team from that golden era and my formative Boro-watching years. UTB

BORO 0 – 1 BIRMINGHAM CITY
AYRESOME PARK, 1975
ANDY WILLOUGHBY

There were earlier cup and reserve games when I was really little but I remember nothing about them except running around people's legs and messing about with my cousin. The first I remember properly is playing Birmingham City at Ayresome Park in the cup in the 1975 season. I was with my dad and my Uncle Brian in the seats behind the goal. I'd convinced my dad I was really into it now. We lost 1- 0. I was excited to see David 'Spike' Armstrong putting in his legendary in-swinging corners, seeing Graeme Souness and Bobby Murdoch passing it around with style, and seeing how big 'Big John' Hickton and how hard Stuart Boam was. I was disappointed we lost and thought we were unlucky. I seem to remember a very young Trevor Francis playing for them and thinking he was going to be a great player, and also more than anything seeing how truly great a player my hero Willie Maddren was, how gracefully he moved for a defender and how he read the game. I guess it was unusual that my hero wasn't a striker. I liked John Craggs a lot too and I mostly played right back later at school. I could name the whole team and really was excited to see them all. I remember really getting into it for the first time and my dad being impressed at how I shouted and joined in the singing as he'd expected me to be overwhelmed. I think he was surprised I didn't disappear nose down into a book halfway through! I went to every game at Ayresome after that till I went away to uni in 1985 except one cup game against Everton due to flu. Anyway, losing didn't put me off! "Next time we'll win, that cup will be ours, next year!"

The eternal dream of hope of the Boro lad.

GETTING IN FOR FREE
AYRESOME PARK, 1959/60
BORO BOY BARI CHOHAN RIP

As a young boy of nine years old at the beginning of the 1959/60 season for Middlesbrough FC in the Second Division of English football, I began my rites of passage to my first ever live game. The ritual encompassed getting into the ground for free. So, I was first initiated by crawling through the legs of many and through the turnstiles at the Boys End.

BORO 0 – 2 READING
RIVERSIDE STADIUM, MARCH 2012
BECCA MORRIS

My first Boro match was in March 2012 when I was twelve years old. It was Boro v Reading, I remember I went with my dad and sat in the North Stand. We lost the game 0-2 but I still thought we played well and really enjoyed it. From that game my first favourite Boro player was Jason Steele because I felt sorry for the amount of stick he was getting from the crowd as I thought he had still made some good saves. I remember loving all the noise and excitement from the crowd. I then went on to love going to the football and got a Season Ticket for the following season and have had one ever since.

LEEDS UNITED 1 – 0 BORO
ELLAND ROAD, OCTOBER 12TH 1985
BERNIE SLAVEN, FORMER BORO PLAYER

I remember facing Leeds at Elland Road and there being a hostile atmosphere due to manager Eddie Gray on the verge or having been sacked – the game itself I think we lost 1-0 from a penalty.

My personal memory was the fitness levels. Don't forget, I had been part time and had been banned from training at Albion while both sides Boro and Leeds were full time. I remember being handed the no 9 shirt and thinking I want 7, which eventually I was handed after asking.

Obviously the first season was tough due to missing Glasgow and adapting to full time training every day. After my first season I felt I settled and started to enjoy it and score goals.

The team I was joining were struggling and eventually relegated and deservedly so. The players simply were not good enough or professional enough. They were messing about at training, cars parked outside the Yellow

Rose in Linthorpe on a Thurs/Fri, totally unprofessional. I would have liked to know what they would have been up to if we were top of the division.

WATCHING WILLIE WHIGHAM
AYRESOME PARK
BILL FELLOWS

My first memories are very vague. But I think I was about thirteen or fourteen when I went to my first match with a friend at Ayresome Park. Was there a Bob End or a family end? I can't remember. We lived in Mill Street, in the Newport area, so we walked there. We were playing Ipswich. The crowd was small for this match. It was the days of Hickton, Maddren, Eric McMordie and Willie Whigham. We stood right behind the goal. Next to us was a family, a dad, with his two young kids who were about eight or nine year old. Willie kept swearing all the time. We could hear him clearly. When the ball was at the other end, the dad with the kids asked Willie to keep his language down… Willie told him to F**K OFF. I couldn't believe it and found it very funny. I have no idea about the score but I will never forget Willie Whigham or my first match.

WEST BROMICH ALBION 2 – 1 BORO
THE HAWTHORNS, SEPTEMBER 3RD 1977
BILLY ASHCROFT, FORMER BORO PLAYER

I remember I didn't have a car at the time so borrowed a crappy mini van and met (Boro manager) John Neal at the country club. I parked it next to Charlie Amer's roller. I was over the moon signing and am still glad to this day I chose Boro.

Debut was WBA away and I drove the van down to West Brom on the day of the game so I could drive back to Wrexham after the match. I was more nervous of the car breaking down than playing the game.

We got battered. It was all a bit of a blur, to be honest, an awful lot to take in. From signing to playing was only a couple of days, so trying to get to know the lads with everything else happening was difficult. I remember Graeme Souness looking after me. He was a great player but also a fantastic bloke. He made sure I got settled. It was a hard game and as I didn't know some of the lads' names I was calling them anything I could think of. I found out what a good bunch of guys I had around me over the next few weeks.

SK BRANN V BORO
BRANN STADIUM, APRIL 1974
BJARTE HJARTØY

SK Brann appointed in 1973 Bill Elliot as coach (we don't have managers in Norway). During his period from 1973 to 1978, he managed to get many English football clubs to Bergen and play against SK Brann.

And I think the first one was Middlesbrough FC in April 1974. I didn't have a favourite English team at that time, so when Middlesbrough came to Brann Stadium I went to the game with a notebook for autographs. I went early and got all the players' (and Jackie Charlton's) autographs. And from that day I was addicted to Middlesbrough FC as my English football club.

It took me 21 years before I travelled over to England and Middlesbrough, but unfortunately that was too late to visit Ayresome Park. But at least it was the Riverside. I was working as a taxi driver and the cab was covered with a Union Jack, as a commercial for the ferry company that sailed between Bergen and Newcastle. So I got a free trip with the ferry and I chose a date (November 25th 1995), when Middlesbrough played Liverpool at the Riverside.

The ferry arrived at Newcastle Friday night and on Saturday at 1pm about fifty of us went down to Middlesbrough by bus. There was no time to pre-drink in a local pub, so we went straight to Riverside Stadium. And what a feeling that was. For the first time ever I was together with other Boro fans. The atmosphere was superb and that Middlesbrough won 2-1 did definitely help for my experience of being at the Riverside for the first time.

Unfortunately, we had to drive back to Newcastle straight after the game, where the ferry actually was waiting for just us to arrive. But of course, I've been back loads of times after this and stayed many nights in

Middlesbrough. So I know Middlesbrough quite well now.

BORO 1 – 1 NOTTINGHAM FOREST
AYRESOME PARK, SATURDAY 10TH OCTOBER 1981
BOB FISCHER

Beery breath, cigar smoke, grass, Deep Heat and Bovril. Those were the smells. Coupled with 'language' – bellowed at high volume – that was very new to me, too. From blokes the size of Wainstones, in sheepskin coats and sagging flat caps. Saturday 10th October, 1981, with Middlesbrough at home to Nottingham Forest. My dad, already (correctly) predicting relegation, reluctantly took me as an early ninth birthday present. "Can I give this one a squeeze?" he asked, shoving me over the turnstiles, effectively also securing me a free ninth birthday present. Still, they were tough times. With my Dad a sporadically-employed builder, our family was effectively living out Boys From The Blackstuff.

I wanted to see Nottingham Forest play. Cloughie was my hero, because he'd sent me a lovely letter and signed photo earlier in the year, when I'd written to his club asking for a replacement for my burst casey. But the Boro bug... well, it didn't quite bite that day, but it certainly nibbled a little. I remember feeling scared, intimidated and – actually – not a little bored. I realised for the first time that there were long, interminable gaps between the goals. And the first Boro goal I ever saw, perversely, was an own goal, nudged into his own net by Forest defender Bryn Gunn, the equaliser in a 1-1 draw. A touch of the contrary that has stayed with me ever since. I still derive just as much pleasure from displays of hapless ineptitude on a football pitch as I do from glittering displays of skill.

But something clearly made an impression, because – a month later – I was back, cheering on Boro to a mesmerising 3-3 draw with Aston Villa, with a late brace from the extraordinary Billy Ashcroft. This time, I chucked in a bit of celebratory 'language' of my own... but only, of course, when my dad was out of earshot.

BORO 0 – 5 HIBERNIAN
AYRESOME PARK, NOVEMBER 27TH 1957
BOB KERR

I can't remember my very first game – early 50s – but the clearest images of a game come from, I think, the Boro's first floodlit game. It was a friendly against Hibs but is there ever such a thing as a friendly between England and Scotland? I remember thinking, "Oh yes, Scot's football is very skilful, but slower than English. We'll overpower them." I'll never forget the impact the lights (although nowhere near as strong as today) had on me. The greenness of the pitch, the whiteness of the lines, and the shirts! Our red, and their green and white. And the game itself! They were so fast and slick. The score I think was 0-5. Only later I was told that their forwards were the Famous Five, legendary figures in Scots football, Smith, Turnbull… I got over the thrashing but never lost that thrill from the lights.

STANDING ON A WOODEN LUNCHBOX TO SEE
AYRESOME PARK
BRIAN LAVERICK

Unfortunately I cannot remember who Boro were playing at my first game but it was back in the Stan Anderson era. All I remember from it was being mesmerised by the away supporters chanting. My dad made me a wooden lunch box that I stood on to get a better view and then at half time opened up for my sandwiches and I always had the old Oxo drinks that they sold and then got the programme out to see scores of other games. Remember the score display? You had to use your programme to know which fixture scores they were.

I always went in the Bob End and even had one of those rattles.

The fixture that stood out for me as a teenager was the FA Cup quarter final against Wolves. Over 40,000 people there and buzzing with atmosphere. As you know, not the result we wanted though.

BORO V LIVERPOOL
AYRESOME PARK, FRIENDLY, 1970
CAROLINE WALKER

My first Boro match was a friendly against Liverpool at Ayresome Park in 1970. I was thirteen and my brother would be nine and we were looking for something to do at the weekend and saw an advert in the Gazette for the match. I suppose post 1966 football seemed attractive as did Liverpool, but at the time I knew nothing about Boro. Me, my younger brother and dad went along. I think we won the match – players like Ian St John, Ray Clemence and Emlyn Hughes played. The scary thing is that means that fifty years on from that fateful day I am still hooked on Boro and football. In those fifty years I have been privileged to see the greats play in the flesh: George Best, Lionel Messi and that wonderful Barca team that included Iniesta, Javi, Dani Alves then Neymar, Suarez.

BORO 1 – 1 SPURS
AYRESOME PARK, LEAGUE CUP, OCTOBER 3RD 1972
CHRIS BARTLEY

In the 47 years since, I've seen promotion, relegations and even a few cup finals but nothing quite as memorable as that first game. I can still remember the excitement of the 263 pulling up in Linthorpe Village and seeing the most amazing cosmic floodlights. They shone upon World Cup medal winning hero Nobby Stiles like a Hollywood spotlight. And the pitch. WOW, that beautiful pitch. It was the most vivid colour I've ever witnessed. Every blade of green grass seemed to glisten and sparkle. I was mesmerised. We drew 1-1 thanks to a goal from King John Hickton. I was hooked forever.

BORO 2 – 0 NORWICH
AYRESOME PARK, SATURDAY 30TH MARCH 1968
CHRIS BLOOMFIELD

Okay, my first Boro game, eh? If I remember rightly it was Saturday 30th March 1968 against Norwich City in the (old) 2nd Division; the

Manager was Stan Anderson and we won 2-0, with the scorers being John Hickton and Mike Kear. The attendance was just over 10,000, sufficiently modest enough for my dad to get a parking spot on Kensington Road, close to Ayresome Park Road and Clive Road and our ultimate destination of the South Stand Upper where my dad had a Season Ticket and who on that day got me in as a 'squeeze' for nothing! As well as the great 'Big John' on duty that day, other notable players were Willie Whigham, Gordon Jones, Frank Spraggon, Dickie Rooks, Derrick Downing and Eric McMordie – now, those were the days!

BORO 0 – 2 CARLISLE UNITED
AYRESOME PARK, AUGUST 20TH 1974
CHRIS HICKS

I went to boarding school in Carlisle in 1973, and Jack Charlton's team ran away with the Division 2 title in the 1973/74 season, which made it that much easier to identify with my home town whilst I was away. The first Boro game I went to was at Ayresome Park at the start of the next season, our first run in the top division in my living memory. Ironically it was against Carlisle United, who surprisingly topped the division at the start of that season. We lost 2-0 at home, but bizarrely won the away fixture 1-0 only a couple of weeks later. At a guess, the team was: Platt, Craggs, Spraggon, Boam, Maddren, Murdoch, Souness, Mille, Hickton, Foggon, Armstrong.

BORO 4 – 0 DARLINGTON
AYRESOME PARK, DECEMBER 27TH 1966
CHRIS JOSEPH

As founder of the Middlesbrough Supporters Forum you would probably expect me to remember everything about my first ever Boro match but you're wrong!

My dad, Basil (RIP) took me along when I was about eight years old. Both my parents were originally from India and dad had been a Chief Engineer in the Indian Merchant Navy back in the fifties. During that time one of his ships was once beached off Teesside. As the sailors had to await a specific tide to refloat the ship, they had come ashore to Middlesbrough and some, including my dad, had watched football at Ayresome Park. Dad and his family migrated to Sheffield some years later but dad had never expected to eventually move to Teesside where he became Standards Engineer of ICI Billingham.

I was being given a special treat, but I didn't know what. After a hearty meal my mum insisted I wrapped up well and my dad produced two polythene bags which I had to put over my socks before I put my feet into my wellies (insulation from the cold!). My mum had knitted me a red and white scarf. My dad and I travelled by bus to Middlesbrough and, under instructions not to let go of my dad's hand, we walked briskly towards Ayresome Park.

I could see the glow above the stadium from a distance with its huge stands silhouetted by four massive pylons topped by the tall illuminated floodlights. Despite the large meal, my dad treated me to a hot dog (with onions and ketchup!). I was struck by the hustle and bustle of the people and I'd never seen so many people heading in one direction at once. I was amazed by the sheer size of the stadium which only became obvious as we emerged into the South Stand. I was astonished by the fact that somewhere that large could be lit up so brightly and as I emerged into the stand, my nostrils were filled with the strong aroma of the chlorophyll from the freshly cut grass, a smell I enjoy to this day.

The crowd was singing and swaying and we were packed in like sardines. My dad held onto me throughout. I remember the roar of the crowd as the match kicked off, but to this day I do not know who we were playing! I managed to glimpse three of the four goals we scored that day and screamed as loud as I'd ever been allowed to with every goal. The oohs, the aahs, the highs and lows of emotion I felt, the singing, the chanting and the noise of the crowd were exhilarating. It was fantastic and... I was hooked! I found Ayresome, absolutely awesome! I have followed the Boro ever since.

AWAY TO LINCOLN CITY
SINCIL BANK, 1992
CHRIS LOFTHOUSE

As first game stories go I'm rather proud of this one. Back in 1992 I was a footy mad six year old who was lucky enough to live over the road from one of his Boro heroes, Gary Parkinson. I was probably still too little to brave Ayresome at the time and hadn't yet seen the boys in red first hand. During that summer holiday I joined my grandparents and an uncle on the family canal boat and somehow we ended up in glamorous Lincoln. Yes, I know, amazing. We happened to be there the day Boro came to town, the Premier League new boys warming up against little old Lincoln City. Myself and our Craig went down to Sincil Bank to wave the boys off the coach. Parky recognised me, the crazy little lad from Ingleby, as he got off the coach and darted into the ground only to emerge with a pair of tickets to my first ever real life football match. It's been a gesture and a memory I've remembered fondly since, probably more and more as the years pass. We got shanked that day, I think, but I didn't care. Parky, thanks for setting me off on a lifetime of Boro.

GIANT FLOODLIGHTS REACHING UP TO THE SKY
AYRESOME PARK, 1954
CHRIS MADDREN

My first visit was in 1954 when I was seven and older brother Dave eight years old. Boro had just been relegated from Division 1 and the legendary Wilf Mannion had left the club. It would be a further twenty years before returning to the top flight and our younger brother William would be a key part in that success.

As young children my dad Vince would talk to us about Mannion, Camsell, Hardwick and many more heroes. Our first introduction to live football was when he took us to the old wooden stadium on Belasis Avenue belonging to the Synthonia for who he turned out for a handful of times before the war as a tough tackling no nonsense full back, but shift work curtailed it.

Anyway, the time had come to go to his beloved Boro at Ayresome Park so dad took us over the Tranny and walked up Linthorpe Road towards Albert Park with more and more spectators joining as we went. We turned into Ayresome Park Road and wow, what a sight, those giant floodlights reaching up to the sky and the large stand like nothing had we seen before. Dad put us in the queue for the Boys End and he went to the adult entrance to the Bob End.

We raced up the concrete steps high up into the boys' enclosure and were so excited to see the magnificent stadium and green pitch out there. Dad met us near the bottom of the Boys End wall and lifted us over into the Bob End amongst the grown ups and sat us on a barrier for a better view. The blue haze of smoke through the rays of the floodlights from all of the smoking was a sight to see.

The match got underway to huge applause and our hearts were racing in anticipation. When there was a lull in the atmosphere, suddenly this great booming voice come out from the North Stand terracing shouting,

"Come on, you Boooooooro," to much applause and laughter from the home crowd. Dad said it was a West Indian gentleman called Astor who was a comedian doing the clubs in the area and the Yorkshire mining towns. Some say that Charlie Williams copied his act.

I remember our goalie called Ugolini, and Delapenha on the right wing who had the hardest shot in football and burst the side net from a penalty and the ref said it missed!

We saw Delapenha bursting down the right wing towards the Holgate End with the full back with him on his shoulder, when he stopped the ball and carried on running with the full back alongside unaware that the ball had gone. It was hilarious.

The Bob End remained my favourite until the mid-1960s when the Holgate End became more popular. I would stand in the north west corner just inside of the canopy in case it rained but well away from the loud chanting and swearing. I started taking my two children Simon and Jill there, going early to get a spot at the barrier only for a six foot four bloke to come in at five to three and stand in front.

They carried on being loyal supporters and all became Season Ticket holders when the Riverside Stadium opened.

TESTIMONIAL MATCHES
AYRESOME PARK
CLAIRE BOWDLER

My first game was at Ayresome Park. I went to Clayton Blackmore's Testimonial and then my second game was Stephen Pears' Testimonial, the last game at Ayresome Park.

I don't remember much about that game to be honest. I wasn't into football at the time. My dad took me to the game. I took an interest in Manchester United for a brief time. Beckham, Scholes, Neville brothers, Lee Sharpe… But I remember more from the last game at Ayresome Park.

BORO V SUNDERLAND
AYRESOME PARK, DECEMBER 26TH 1973
CRAIG LIGHTFOOT

One of my faintest memories of going to watch the Boro at the age of ten was a Boxing Day game against Sunderland in the 1973/74 season. I went with my dad and uncle and the Holgate End was that packed and with me being small I didn't get to see much of the game but at least we won.

One of my early games that I can remember was a 1st leg League Cup Semi-Final game against Man City. It was a night match and we were in the stand with the concrete slabs opposite the Holgate End. We won the game 1-0 with John Hickton scoring the winner, unfortunately we lost the 2nd leg at Maine Road 4-0. I think they won the final 2-1 against Newcastle. I also remember the home game against Newcastle that season with us leading 3-1 until the dying minutes only for them to score two very late goals to draw level. I can remember us having a very good team at the time under Jack Charlton and also a strong team in John Neal's era when I went to the games regularly.

BORO 2 – 1 QPR
AYRESOME PARK, OCTOBER 23RD 1982
DAN GILGAN

I was a nine-year-old kid when I attended my first Middlesbrough match. Earlier in the year I had fallen in love with football as I watched the 1982 World Cup on our tiny 14-inch television. In the months leading up to the tournament, me and my school friends had enthusiastically collected Panini's España '82 sticker album. As the faces of the England team gradually populated the double page spread in the album, my excitement at the forthcoming tournament built. After an early flurry of excitement with England's 3-1 win over France, the tournament eventually ended in bitter disappointment as Ron Greenwood's team were knocked out of the tournament after a frustrating 0-0 draw with hosts Spain. My teary disappointment at England's World Cup failure would of course become an all too familiar feeling over the coming decades, but that first moment of footballing heartbreak remains fresh in my mind to this day.

Despite the disappointment of España '82,

I was now hooked on the beautiful game. My family lived in a little terraced house which was a ten minute walk from Ayresome Park and on Saturday afternoons, as my brother and I kicked a football around the back yard, we could hear the sound of the crowd. Listening to the Ayresome songs drifting into the yard brought the grown-up world of professional football tantalisingly close and we soon began begging our dad to take us to a game. Boro had been relegated from the old First Division the previous season and it was a pretty grim time for the club, but when Malcolm Allison was announced as the new manager, dad gave into the pressure and promised to take us to the next home game.

It was a Saturday afternoon in late October 1982, and as we walked to the ground, dad recounted his own childhood memories of Boro's 1967 promotion game, explaining that the crowd was packed in so tightly that fans spilled onto the pitch. He remembered singing, "Give us a goal John O'Rourke," before kick-off and celebrating O'Rourke's hat trick as Boro beat Oxford United to win promotion back to the Second Division. Dad's memories put our first visit to Ayresome into a broader historical context, and I felt the nostalgia of family history adding to the anticipation of my first game.

As we queued up to get into the stadium, I listened to blokes chatting about the game and breathed in the smells of hot-dogs and fried onions, cigarette smoke and beery breath. When we got into the ground, I was struck by the sight of the smooth green pitch which contrasted the vibrant red corrugated roof of the Holgate End opposite us. Just before kick-off, the new manager Malcolm Allison came onto the pitch and waved to the crowd who warmly applauded the new boss. Despite the arrival of a new manager, the stadium was sparsely populated and the meagre crowd of around 7,000 was a far cry from that game in the 1960s that dad had spoken of.

We sat on the wall at the back of the small family terrace which ran along the length of the pitch behind the East End goal, and as the match kicked off I remember the roar of the crowd behind us. Despite the poor attendance, the fans in the corner terrace above us made plenty of noise, chanting, "Come on Boro" and "Away the lads," every time the team came forward. Other chants that came from those fans in the Bob End and the far off Holgate End at the other end of the pitch included the kind of 'industrial' language that was never heard in our house and my father shook his head to show us his disapproval.

In all honesty, my memories of the actual match are sketchy to say the least, but I clearly remember watching Boro's keeper Jim Plat in his green shirt guarding the goal in front of us. Platt and Boro winger Terry Cochrane both played for Northern Ireland and were familiar faces from my España '82 sticker album. Despite the presence on the pitch of Boro's World Cup stars, it was another player who really impressed: a skinny young lad on the wing who had the skill to leave opposition defenders looking confused as he ran past them with the ball. His name was Stephen Bell and his pacey skills were one highlight of an otherwise rather ordinary team. Every time he got on the ball the crowd cheered their approval, and I remember the cry of "Go on, Son!" from blokes stood nearby as he ran with the ball.

As the afternoon light faded, the tall floodlights came on and illuminated the pitch, adding another fascinating visual memory to the afternoon. Strangely, I couldn't actually tell you how the goals were scored that afternoon, but I can certainly remember the huge roar of the crowd as Boro's two goals went in. We won 2-1 that day with the goals being scored by Heine Otto and Irving Nattrass. As I walked home that cold Saturday evening with my dad and brother, I felt proud to have watched my first game. It was the beginning of a long journey as a Middlesbrough fan and little did that nine-year-old boy know quite what he was letting himself in for.

BORO 2 – 0 PORTSMOUTH
RIVERSIDE STADIUM, MAY 3RD 2008
DANA MALT

It was towards the end of the 2007/08 season, the second from last home game in fact. May

3rd, 2008. Boro were playing Portsmouth. It was a strange time to get into supporting Boro actually; the club's halcyon days were firmly in the past and we were witnessing the sprouting of the fall. I remember the Riverside being half empty (something I got used to as the years passed), and as a result the atmosphere was subdued.

Tuncay – one of the scorers that day – immediately stood out to me. His endeavour and work rate is what caught the eye. As a fan, that's the bare minimum of what we want to see. Those greasy locks and sort of casually loose fitted kit as well. To seven-year-old Dana, he was an icon!

We won the game 2-0 and it secured our status as a Premier League club. The game after that, only the second I had attended, was the 8-1 drubbing of Man City. I refer to it as the catfish of all games as I was in for quite the shock with what happened next...

BORO 3 – 1 PLYMOUTH ARGYLE
AYRESOME PARK, APRIL 30TH 1988
DANIEL COCHRAN

I wasn't a big football fan until I started going to games, and I certainly don't remember begging my dad to see the Boro. In fact, I've a nagging feeling I was dragged to Ayresome against my will. My first taste of the magical matchday atmosphere: Plymouth Argyle, who (alongside Notts County with the peach-fuzz red hair of Tommy Johnson) I seem to remember us playing every other week.

It was April 30th 1988 so I'd have been five years old. Before the game we went to Inn off the Park on Linthorpe Road, a place which in my mind occupies a similar space as the Cantina in Star Wars: A wretched hive of scum and villainy where I could eat as many dry roasted peanuts and pork scratchings as I wanted. I could even, on occasion, indulge in a bottle of Britvic 55 – the juvenile equivalent of a fine single malt.

My only actual memory of the game was a formative one. Stuart Ripley (aka 'Skin-em Rippers') lived at the bottom of my road and was everyone in Acklam's favourite player. When he got married a few years later, the local kids surrounded the church on The Oval to congratulate him (he even got a guard of honour from the Junior Reds). Ripley became my first and (until Uwe) definitive Boro hero when he managed to capitalise on an almighty cock-up between the Plymouth goalkeeper and defender to thread the ball home – agonisingly slowly – from a near impossible angle. Subsequent research has determined that we won 3-1, but that one image is the only one that stuck.

Although the Plymouth game was at the back end of a promotion-winning season (and despite all our 90s top-tier heroics), to me we'll always be a second-tier club. I don't mean that as a slight, it's just the mental box I put us into. When I imagine Boro, we're playing Sheff Utd and Swindon at Ayresome, not Man Utd at the Riverside, and that's entirely due to games like this.

I've watched it back and Hamilton scored a screamer (with somersault celebration) that entirely failed to register with me. Memory, eh?

Also it was the first time I realised I was colour-blind.

BORO 3 – 3 ASTON VILLA
AYRESOME PARK, DECEMBER 1988
DANIEL GRAY

I was seven years old when my dad gave me a choice: Middlesbrough, the team closest to my Stockton birthplace, or Leeds United, his team. We had moved from Eaglescliffe down to a village near York and not far from his native West Yorkshire.

In December 1988, we went to Ayresome Park to watch Boro. In May 1989, we went to Elland Road to watch Leeds. Boro drew 3-3 against Aston Villa and the floodlights made the pitch look like a cinema screen. Leeds drew 0-0 against Oldham Athletic and afterwards Noel Blake refused to sign my autograph book. The choice was easy. It is impossible to imagine another me, dressed in white and not red. Boro were my frequently disappointing, occasionally delightful destiny.

Of that Villa game, I remember what you are supposed to remember as a first time fan: we walked behind a scampering horde of men in jeans, peeled off down an alleyway copied from the opening credits of Coronation Street, queued towards a turnstile that my dad lifted me over, climbed some weathered steps between shabby mounds of earth and went in, in to what JB Priestley called an 'altogether more splendid kind of life'. Once more, dad hoisted me, this time so that I could sit on a crush barrier at the back of the Holgate End. I can still close my eyes and see that platoon of heads facing the pitch, a few thousand buoys bobbing in a cantankerous sea.

Everything else is colour and scent: the luminous green of the pitch, the blood red of Boro's shirts, darkening skies tricked pale by the floodlights; cigarettes like those my grandad smoked and Teesside's oddly homely chemical vapours. Of the football, I remember the hedonism after each Boro goal went in, and I remember the sheer girth of Gary Hamilton's thighs, obvious even from the back of the Holgate.

BORO 5 – 5 SCOTTISH INTERNATIONAL XI
AYRESOME PARK, WILLIE MADDREN'S TESTIMONIAL, MAY 9TH 1978
DAVE ALLAN

I was a relatively late starter as a Boro fan. My first Boro match should have been the FA Cup quarter-final against Orient in 1978 but my sister refused to take me, despite my begging and tears. As it turned out, Billy Ashcroft scored a hat trick in what turned out to be my first game soon afterwards. My dad took me to Ayresome Park for the first and I sat in the rather sedate Clive Road Stand for what also turned out to be the last time for Willie Maddren's testimonial. The match was an amazing 5-5 draw so nothing like the 42 years since then!

Suffering a long-term injury that would force him to retire from the game, Willie kicked off the match, waved to the fans then left the pitch. Sadly, it was the only time I saw the great man kick a ball but many years later I'd have the honour of ghostwriting his autobiography, Extra Time. I remember looking around with awe at Ayresome Park and flicking through the pages of a programme I'd end up editing 16 years later during Boro's last season at Ayresome. And then there was the weird beverage experience. At half-time dad asked me if I wanted a drink. I expected him to come back with a can of pop. Instead he returned with what seemed to the eleven-year-old me to be a steaming plastic cup of gravy. I didn't try Bovril again for many years!

That summer roared on Scotland at the 1978 World Cup (I knew Don Masson had played for Boro) but it was my Boro love affair that was up and running.

Funnily enough I've just realised that the first league match I have any memory of is Terry Cochrane's debut the following season. I'd definitely gone to the earlier games that season but can't recall anything about them. Then Cochrane arrived. I'd never seen anyone with such skill. And soon after I remember rushing into my house and shouting, "Dad, Boro won 7-2!" The day Micky Burns scored 4 v Chelsea. My early hero was actually Craig Johnston, loved him to bits.

BORO 3 – 3 NEWCASTLE
AYRESOME PARK, JANUARY 1976
DAVE BROWN

I don't really have a memory of my first game at Ayresome Park. I remember games on the Rec near our house, in our little back garden in Teesville, or the play ground matches and games for my old primary school in South Bank always pretending to be David Mills or Souness. I even still have some of my treasured old Football Cards. You didn't have swaps back then, in our school you had to win them by spinning your card like a frisbee at the toilet block wall. Closest to the wall wins all. But not my first ever Boro game?

I don't remember the line ups, nor the opposition or even the scores from games I do remember going to. What I do have is what most people have, a 'feeling' of everything mixed into one. I know my dad took me, then my brothers. I have a feeling of the sounds, the smells and the tastes. But most of all the emotion of the whole event is what has stayed with me. I asked my brother Maca when my first game was and straight away he said, "Jan 1976

Boro v Newcastle 3-3, week of your birthday."
Bloody hell, what a game not to remember.
Even now after watching it on You Tube it stirs
no memories in fact it leaves me cold. Actually
I was in the Beechwood and Easterside Club
recently and my ex-brother-in-law was talking
about this very game. About how cold it was,
about how when getting beat the Toon fans
kept on singing and then the heartbreak of the
equaliser right at the death. Loads of passion
great atmosphere and all that.

"Do you remember that one, Dave?"

"No, I think I only remember the wins,
Ron."

"You won't remember many then."

"Nope."

BORO 2 – 2 LIVERPOOL
AYRESOME PARK, 1957
DAVE BUDD

Memories of my first Boro match are hazy. It
was against Liverpool in 1957. My dad and I
would have got the United 63 bus to the park
gates. We may have called at grandad's house

in Warwick Street close to Ayresome Park. I found out later that my grandad knew some of the players in the 1920s and 1930s, though he rarely went to the match.

My dad was more interested in cricket than football. I recall that he gave me a choice when we were on holiday in Scarborough. I could go to the joys of Peasholm Park with my mam and younger brother or go to watch Yorkshire. I think he was really pleased and, perhaps, surprised that I chose the cricket. My memories of the match consist of the amazement of being a few yards from Len Hutton as he strolled round the boundary.

My first Boro match memory is mainly a feeling, rather than specific details of the 2-2 draw. It was difficult for me to see much anyway standing under the main stand. This thought came back to me when my daughters, and later my granddaughter, went to their first games.

It was a few seasons later when I became a regular in the Bob End and by then I had received the lifetime sentence which has provided so many memories since.

BORO 4 – 1 CARDIFF
AYRESOME PARK, JANUARY 11TH 1958
DAVE CONNOR

January 11th 1958, Cardiff at home, won 4-1, Peacock 3, Harris Penalty. Me dad Tommy Connor took me. I was eleven at the time. Squeeze in, lift over the turnstile at the Bob End. The team was Taylor, Bilcliff, Brown, Harris, Phillips, Birbeck, Day, McLean, Clough, Peacock, Holliday. As we were walking home, I remember saying to dad, "I thought you told me we were going to see Cloughie?" He did not score on the night but he got 42 from 42 for the season.

Extra Stuff: The forward line that night only played 11 league and 2 cup games together but it is talked about as the greatest forward line in Boro history.

BORO 2 – 0 OXFORD
AYRESOME PARK, JANUARY 1969
DAVE ROBERTS

I'm told the first game I attended was Boro's 2-0 defeat of Oxford at Ayresome back in

January 1969, but as I was a five-year-old it's hard to remember. Harry Glasper's Complete Record, bless it, tells me Jonny Crossan and Big John Hickton completed the double over the Us in front of me, but sorry, it's far too far back, I'm far too old, it's not even a blur.

The first real game I can remember came just before Christmas in 1971. It was the trip to Boothferry Park where we put three past Hull only to lose 4-3. The overriding memory of the old ground was a big car park, okay a field, out the back of the stand, a bit of a strange thing to remember it has to be said. I took a camera to record Millsie grab two with a flicked header and left foot rocket, but Craggsie stole the show, hammering the ball high into the roof of the net from what, I probably exaggerate, seemed an impossible angle. I think 'Typical Boro' started for me that day, 2-3 up only to concede two late to lose.

Sadly the Evening Gazette had nothing to worry about from my photographic skills as players looked like ants in the old black and white pics, but at least the stands turned out okay because they were pretty imposing. The creme de la creme was Stewie Boam stopped for a quick snap, in black and white, the song was re-written to 6ft 2, eyes of light grey, but he still became an instant hero.

BEING WEANED OFF MAN UTD
AYRESOME PARK, 1972/73
DAVE ROBSON

The details are sketchy of my first Boro match, although I know it was in the 1972/73 season. I know where I'll have been watching it from, too – a curious spot in the North Stand Upper, at the Holgate End, just beneath where the temperamental electronic scoreboard would soon appear, a scoreboard which, with its riot of broken bulbs and bad connections, usually only gave the merest of clues as to how other games were going.

My dad, you see, was the gateman in charge of 'B Door' and, eager to wean me off George Best's Man Utd, he took me with him to a Boro game – yes, it's all his fault – and, with the gateman's office's permission, I was allowed in for free. So that he knew where I was, dad plonked me in the far corner of the stand with his colleague's son. Our 'brief' was to watch the gate and stairs connecting the upper and lower enclosures in case of interlopers.

We did no such thing, of course – we watched the match. But because our dads had to be there early, we'd also watch the ground filling up, which became a major part of the matchday experience. From Bernard Gent cranking up 'Radio Ayresome' and the players coming out for their warm-ups to the Holgate faithful cramming together in the centre to sing all sorts of unsavoury songs, I was hooked from the start. It was even more exciting in B Door because that's where complementary ticket holders sat – from the occasional Club Fiesta celebrity to the downcast injured or fringe players who'd failed to make the final 12.

I'd have almost certainly been there when John Hickton bagged a hat trick in the final game of the 1972/73 season, a 3-2 home win over Orient in front of less than 8,000. But when Jack Charlton took over from Stan Anderson, any thoughts of me returning to the Man Utd fold were banished for ever…

and I know for a fact I was at his first game in charge, the 0-2 night match home defeat to Fulham. Thinking I wasn't that bothered, dad drove us away from the ground before the match ended, probably muttering something about, "You'd better get used to that, son." Well, not in that season I didn't, as Charlton's Champions swept most opponents aside – although, in my childish naivety, I thought it would always be that way...

BORO 2 – 1 PORTSMOUTH
AYRESOME PARK, MARCH 7TH 1970
DAVEY NORTH

I can remember my first Boro match. I remember the score was a 2-1 against Portsmouth on March 7th 1970 (I googled the date) which will make me six years old. My uncle took me, and in time honoured fashion back then, I climbed over the turnstile. At the time I 'supported' Wolves just because I liked the colour of their kit. 90 minutes later I was a Boro fan and John Hickton was my hero. However, the thing I remember over anything was my first view of the pitch. I'd never seen anything so green in my life. Strange how that memory has always stayed with me.

BORO 2 – 0 WIMBLEDON
AYRESOME PARK, NOVEMBER 1992
DAVID BATES

At the age of nine, a dark, cold and rainy Saturday in November 1992 was when I first encountered the magic of a childhood visit to Ayresome Park. Although my overall memory of the day is hazy, I can picture brief snapshots of the experience like it happened yesterday. I honestly can't recall any of the walk to the ground; in my mind's eye, one minute we're climbing out of the car in the Hill Street Centre, the next we're inside the ground, walking up the jaded concrete steps from the concourse behind the goal in the East End. But I will never forget the moment we reached the top and my eyes were met by the dazzling, luminous green Ayresome turf in full 'widescreen vision' before me. To be there, live, was one of the most exciting things that had ever happened to me.

Boro's opposition were Wimbledon and all the talk beforehand had focused on Vinnie Jones, who a few days previously had been slapped with a fine and threatened with a long-term ban for 'glorifying violence' in his pre-Christmas stocking-filler video 'Soccer's Hardmen'. Predictably enough, with the eyes of the world on him, Jones was fired up for the occasion and so was the small Ayresome Park crowd. The first half was goalless but packed with the kind of drama that had me hooked instantly: having already shoulder-charged Stephen Pears and tangled with Jon Gittens in the resulting melee, in a short passage of play Jones clattered Derek Whyte, snapped the heels of Willie Falconer and then completely upended John Hendrie in a brutal two-foot lunge. I can picture it vividly as Hendrie, about a foot shorter than Jones, instantly leapt to his feet and grabbed him by the throat, before being pulled away by a throng of players. I was absolutely mesmerised.

Boro eventually ran out 2-0 winners. John Hendrie, already my lifelong hero, scored a brilliant chip which was initially ruled out for offside but then allowed after consultation between the officials; cue pandemonium, with Jones leading a mob of Wimbledon players to surround the linesman, egged on by manager Joe Kinnear. Then, just minutes later, Chris Morris prodded home a scrappy goal to seal victory, and the whole place erupted. What an afternoon… after all this, it was safe to say I was now a Boro fan for life.

WE WON…
AYRESOME PARK
DEAN LANGSTAFF

I have been racking my brain and spoke to the parents, and I think I was six or seven. None of us can remember who it was against but I remember we won, we won the first three times I went, not many can say that. I remember sitting on the resting bar in the old standing terraces. I remember how the crowd built up a chant every time a goal kick was taken, a dying art in today's game. Everything seemed so big and I was overjoyed when we scored.

BORO 2 – 1 NOTTINGHAM FOREST
RIVERSIDE STADIUM
GABRIEL LANGSTAFF

Gabriel was five. Lukas Jutkiewicz scored the winner, not long after we had signed him. He thinks we won 2-1. We took the lead,they equalised and then Lukas got a winner. It was against Nottingham Forest. We went on Nathan Stephenson's Season Ticket. Gabriel loved it. He was shocked at how loud it was and how many people were there.

BORO 1 – 1 SPURS
RIVERSIDE STADIUM, FA CUP, JANUARY 4TH 2020
HUGO LANGSTAFF

Hugo's first game was the Tottenham cup game this season. He was surprised when we scored as he expected Tottenham to beat us. He really, really loved it. He was aged six.

BORO V SCARBOROUGH
AYRESOME PARK, SEPTEMBER 1994
DEBBIE DUNCAN

September 1994, Boro v Scarborough. My sister and I were staying with my aunty and uncle for a few days while mum and dad were away. My uncle really wanted to go to the match, and he could go but on one condition, that he took us with him. So off we went in the rain. The two players I remember most were Hignett and Mustoe (even though it was a Wilkinson hat trick). We were thirteen years old, and it was the most expensive trip away for mum and dad as it cost them annual Season Tickets for us both. Mum later joined us in the North stand at the Riverside.

BORO 3 – 1 SHEFFIELD UNITED
AYRESOME PARK, APRIL 20TH 1957
DEREK AGAR

My first Boro match was on April 20th 1957, when we beat Sheffield United 3-1. Our Uncle Joe, who lived in Chapel Row, Loftus, picked me up from our house in Ormesby and took me in his motorcycle combo.

Uncle Joe was a very funny bloke and was a local football referee, and he was a war hero. He won the Military Medal for leading his men crawling through a minefield in North Africa. I think Uncle Joe cottoned on to me because of our mutual interest in football, which our dad didn't have at that time. Eventually our dad became more interested in the Boro, but when he was on duty as a policeman at Ayresome Park, he could come back home and not know the score!

That April day we parked up somewhere off The Palladium and legged it to the ground. It took an age, but on the way everyone seemed to be talking about Jimmy Hagan and how it would be the last time to see him. Of course, then there was no televised football, so often the only way you would know what opposition star players looked like would be through newspapers or fag cards. Jimmy Hagan was actually from the North East but became a Sheffield United hero.

Despite the endless walk, once we got in the

Bob End, halfway up behind the goal, I loved everything about it – the view, the lush green grass, the nets, the corner flags, the noise of the crowd, the thwack of the meaty tackles, the swearing, everything. Cloughie scored and his future managerial mate Peter Taylor was in goal, specialising in mighty throws from his area into the opposition half. The Irish leprechaun, Arthur Fitzsimons, was at inside left, and Welsh international wing half Bill Harris put away two pennas. I was only little so I had to sit on a concrete barrier, getting down from time to time and having to jump up and down or peer round people to see. I noticed that lots of the blokes had mucky faces, presumably because they'd gone straight from the 6-2 shift to the match.

When we got back and our dad asked what it was like, Uncle Joe and I answered with one word each and at the same time. I said, "Great", he said, "Sh*te." I think he must have been a founder member of the Chicken Run mentality whereby praise and optimism are shunned, to protect against age-old and almost-inevitable disappointment and recurring let-down.

Little did I know at the time, but I was to spend most of my life in Sheffield, having gone to university there and not quite made it back. Through playing in the local snooker league I befriended a man who was Jimmy Hagan's next-door neighbour, so he passed on my story to him. His return messages used to ask about George Hardwick and Wilf Mannion.

I'm still a season-ticket holder at Boro, but living in Sheffield I often have to fight our corner. I usually find that mention of Boro 6 United 0 – with a Stuart Ripley hat trick – or Boro 8 Wednesday 0 – with a Graeme Souness hat trick – effectively settles things down...

That first match of mine was followed two days later by a 7-2 win over Huddersfield, with Cloughie netting four. That season was also the one that started Boro's incredible FIVE consecutive league wins at Anfield, again with Clough goals to the fore.

That first live match was not long after I watched my first match on telly, in a mate's house in our street. It was the 1956 cup final, in which Bert Trautmann broke his neck but carried on in goal for Manchester City, who beat Birmingham. By coincidence, years later when I was in Spain on the east coast, I met a writer called Ian Govan, who was freelance but contributed mainly football articles to, amongst others, The Guardian and When Saturday Comes. I drank with him, talked a lot and he invited us back to his house. In the middle of a barbecue there he ushered me upstairs, unlocked a filing cabinet and said, "Here, I know you'll be interested in this – hold it for a while," and he put in my hand a medal from the 1956 FA Cup Final!

His dad played in the final for Birmingham when they lost to Manchester City. Dad, called Alex Govan, scored 30 goals in a season from the wing, including five hat tricks, notably three of them in the space of ten days – still a top-league record in England! In 1956 Birmingham were the first to reach Wembley having played all of their games away, and they used to entertain themselves and relieve tension by singing on the team bus. Alex's contribution, being from Glasgow, was Harry Lauder's 'Keep Right On to the End of the Road!' The Birmingham fans caught wind of this when the players opened the windows on the team bus, and made it their theme tune, and of course it still is. Ian died in 2012, but his dad was just short of 87 when he died a couple of years later. Ian told me that Harry Lauder wrote the song for his son, who was killed in the trenches in the First World War.

CLOUGH SEEMED QUITE GOOD
AYRESOME PARK
DEREK DENT

I would have been eight when my dad first took me to Ayresome Park. We were now the proud owners of one of the first cars in our street so it was easy to get there. He drove round to the Synthonia club to meet two of his brothers and one of his friends, and I waited in the car while he had a drink with them before driving us all to Middlesbrough over the Newport Bridge. I was hoping it would go up because I enjoyed that when it happened – not very often unfortunately.

We parked in St Barnabas' Road then walked

along to the South Stand which was my dad's spot. I got a lift over the turnstile and my dad took me down to the wall next to the pitch and sat me there to watch the game. We always went about midway between the goal-line and the halfway line towards the Holgate. I remember being amazed by the number of people there and the noise they made – the sense of excitement was palpable. I was now part of something I'd never experienced before.

I really don't remember much about the match itself – who we played, what the score was, – but I do remember some of the players I saw that day and many times afterwards. There was this chap called Clough who seemed quite good, then there was another called Day who moved faster than anyone I'd ever seen but the one that most sticks in my mind was Eddie Holliday who just appeared to trick his way past people whenever he wanted. He became the player I always wanted to see.

BORO V BOLTON
AYRESOME PARK, 1994
ROBIN DENT

I can't really remember my first game! I have vague memories of Ayresome Park itself, mostly of being in the stand when they announced the name of the new stadium and the disappointment and frustration of fans around us that they would go with something so bland as 'Riverside Stadium'!

Sadly, couldn't tell you who played, the result or score!

Note added by father, Derek Dent: I have found a ticket for that game on which Robin wrote '1st football match'. It was for a game against Bolton in 1994 and we were in the East Stand. He was eight then as I thought that my dad had got it right in judging when I was the right age for my first game.

BORO V SWANSEA
AYRESOME PARK, FA CUP, JANUARY 1995
DOMINIC SHAW

It's funny how the most random things stick in your mind. I remember showing my next door neighbour my new Boro shirt before I set off with my dad. I remember the stench of fried onions as I walked into the ground. And I remember being struck by how orange Swansea's shirts were. My first game was January in 1995 – the shock FA Cup defeat to the lowly Swans. If I'm honest, I don't remember the details of the game meaning that much to me at the time, I was more interested in the bag of midget gems I was armed with and devouring. And John Hendrie's goal that proved to be a consolation is a memory of watching my season review videos again and again and again rather than from the night itself. Still, though, the defeat didn't put me off. Neither did the onions. I remember being desperate for more. On reflection, I do wish I was older at the time to really appreciate the joys of Ayresome Park. I was brought up on a diet of Boro success, though my dad made sure I was well aware of what had gone before. You'd have thought an FA Cup defeat to lower league Welsh opposition would be a one-off. But then there was Wrexham. And then there was Newport. And Christ, now I'm thinking about Cardiff. Let's leave it there.

BORO 4 – 1 SCARBOROUGH
AYRESOME PARK, SEPTEMBER 1994
DONNA LAW

September 1994, Boro v Scarborough, Wilkinson scored and we won 4 - 1. We went all kitted out in our Boro tops and lots of layers and it was freezing. I remember feeling very excited before going. We got dropped off nearby and walked to the stadium. When we walked in, it was the biggest and loudest stadium I've ever been in. It rained all night and we got soaked. From that moment I was hooked. I remember how loud the singing was and how we all jumped around when we scored.

BORO V MILLWALL
AYRESOME PARK, 1960
JAN BRUNTON,
FORMER COUNCILLOR AND BORO FAN SINCE BIRTH

The first match I ever went to was against Millwall, when I was a child, in 1960, I think. My dad took me to Ayresome Park, and the Millwall supporters threw pennies at us! I remember thinking what awful people they were. But the clearest memory is seeing the pitch for the first time… in colour, as we only had a black and white TV at home… it was amazing!

Note: More than three decades later, Jan's three children, Rachel, Elle, and Paul would also get their first taste of live football watching Boro face-off against Millwall. Again, the match was played at Ayresome Park, this time, in the 1994-1995 season, but it wasn't just the venue that hadn't changed. Rachel, said: "I just remember having to walk really fast through the tunnel because things were being thrown and people [Millwall fans] were swearing!" Interestingly, none can remember much about the games themselves, but the experiences began a life-long love affair with Boro and football in general.

BORO V SPURS
AYRESOME PARK, FA YOUTH CUP FINAL, 1989/90
ELLEN SOWERBY @ELLEN_BORO

I had to ask my dad about this – my mam dropped us off at Ayresome Park to watch the first leg of the FA Youth Cup Final v Spurs in the 1989/90 season. We drew, but I can't remember much about it other than having to balance my backside on the standing barrier things, and not really seeing much of the pitch. We lost the second leg at White Hart Lane, and our family moved away from Teesside not long after that, so I didn't see another game until we'd moved to the Riverside.

LIVERPOOL V BORO
ANFIELD, LEAGUE CUP SEMI-FINAL, JANUARY 1998
FRANCIS ANNETT

My first match was so recent really – late to the party – 1998, January, first leg of the semi-final against Liverpool. We lost quite a tight match but of course won the second leg and went through. Not only my first match supporting Boro, but actually my first match of any sort ever! And at the age of 57. We went by coach and had a meal with Everton at their ground beforehand and walked across to Anfield. What an experience! Paul Merson's goal. I forgot to say the reason we went to the match was the raffle at work when we won the tickets and the whole trip.

BORO 1 – 1 NOTTINGHAM FOREST
RIVERSIDE STADIUM, SATURDAY 16TH MARCH 1996
FRANCIS EMMETT

My first game was in 95, Boro v Forest. I remember sitting on the back row of the West Stand Upper with my dad. Despite being a cameraman regularly at Boro games, he didn't care much for football, he might even have taken a book with him! I remember Forest scoring in a bright yellow away kit, an acrobatic goal of some sorts. I don't think at that point in my life I had ever cheered as much as I did when Mustoe equalised. The stadium erupted, I was jumping up and down and my dad didn't even stand up! That was it, I was hooked. I will always be thankful to my dad for going even when he wasn't in to it himself.

A VISION OF HELL...
GARRY BROGDEN

I won't tell you about my first Boro game (a 1-1 against Forest. Proctor scored for them) but I will tell you about the second, a 0-0 home draw against Sunderland. A dreadful, awful game in terrible conditions, and the vision of hell was only completed when the twenty or so Mackams in the away end set fire to the rubbish on the terracing. As the two teams clogged each other on the pitch, basking in the glow of the flames, I thought, "I'm home."

BORO V CHARLTON
AYRESOME PARK, APRIL 1984
GARY GILL, FORMER BORO PLAYER

I can't remember my first game as a fan and who we played but I used to get a 'squeeze' in the West Stand I think with my dad and used to sit on one of the concrete barriers in front of him. I used to love night games best for the extra atmosphere generated from the lights and the fact that I was allowed to go to bed late! I would spend a lot of the game watching all the fans around me and always remember the smell of Bovril and tobacco everywhere... pipes, cigars, cigarettes... all normal then! I used to love John Hickton's penalties and probably noticed him first on the pitch when I actually got round to watching the football!

My full debut was special because it was my debut, but wasn't memorable as a game as it was an end of season affair with nothing to play for for either team... My full debut was home to Charlton. I'd come on as sub the week before away at Swansea. My parents were at the game and it was an extremely proud moment for me when I ran out in front of them. I'd managed to get there through a lot of hard work and dedication and it hadn't been easy. I'd seen a lot of very good players get released over the years leading up to this and I was beginning to understand how competitive/difficult the professional game was. I was nervous of course and the game was forgettable as a spectacle. I think we won 1-0? Jack Charlton was caretaker/manager, I think. I don't remember how I was told but

I do know that I knew before matchday as I struggled to sleep the night before through a combination of nerves and excitement! The crowd was small, the game was poor, the result was almost irrelevant but the occasion was very special to me and my family who were immensely proud.

BOLTON WANDERERS 3 – 1 BORO
BURNDEN PARK, FEBRUARY 26TH 1983
GARY HAMILTON, FORMER BORO PLAYER

I don't remember much about it to be honest as it was all a blur at the time. The game was against Bolton, away, we lost 3-1. I played left back because Joe Bolton was injured. I never really looked back after that and kind of stuck in the team. I came down from Glasgow on a one day trial and I really liked it especially the Medhurst Hotel which the club owned and players from other areas lived there. So that was very helpful in my decision even though I was still deciding on going to Everton/WBA or Ipswich at the time as that's where I went to train most of my school holidays. And all three wanted to sign me plus numerous clubs in Scotland but my mother wanted me out of Scotland especially Glasgow.

BLACKPOOL 1 – 1 BORO
BLOOMFIELD ROAD, DECEMBER 7TH 1968
GEOFF VICKERS

In 1968 I just turned ten years old and was living in Cheshire. The family had moved from Teesside via Manchester to Northwich but dad always maintained his deep love following the Boro. Whilst my older brothers aligned themselves to the local Man City I was very attached to my dad's team and we made the journey over the Pennines to watch home games in my formative years.

My first game however was an away match in the North West, a Division 2 fixture on December 7th 1968.

We were more than a useful Division 2 side under Stan Anderson. We won way more than we lost and in 1968 we were up in the top four, vying for promotion as we approached Christmas. Blackpool were also challenging so it was with incredible excitement we arrived at Bloomfield Road that day courtesy of a ride in the sidecar of my dad's motorcycle combo. If going to Blackpool in those days wasn't thrilling enough, we spotted the BBC camera vans parked outside. That meant we were to be the feature match on Match of The Day – very unusual given that Div 2 games getting that honour was rare indeed at a time when the programme only showed one match per week.

I remember little of the game itself but I do recall being upset when we went 1-0 down to an Alan Suddick first half strike. I also remember strangely we stood on the side in a small paddock and there was no crowd segregation. Fortunately the Boro goal was recorded by the BBC for prosperity. In the second half, our balding Bobby Charlton look-a-likey centre half Dickie Rooks rose to head a corner home to level and earn a point. 1-1

It was a good point as it turned out. Blackpool were formidable at home. Their manager was FA Cup legend Stan Mortensen and they had players in the team like Tommy Hutchison,

Gordon Milne and the great Jimmy Armfield. Eventually we just missed out on promotion finishing 4th. Blackpool finished 8th.

Boro 11 that day: Maurice Short, Micky Allen, Gordon Jones, Frank Spraggon, Bill Gates, George Kinnell, Dickie Rooks, Dave Chadwick, Derek Downing, Eric McMordie, John Hickton. Att 13, 356

BORO 3 – 1 SHEFFIELD UNITED
AYRESOME PARK, JANUARY 28TH 1969
GEORGE O'NEILL

My father and his evil brother started to take me to Ayresome Park from the beginning of Season 1968/69 when we stood on the South Terrace. Aged ten, I was only just beginning to take an interest in football, had little comprehension of what I was seeing (some would suggest that never changed!) and have no distinct memory of any match prior to a floodlit game on January 28th against a classy Sheffield United team led by their blond god of a midfield maestro, Tony Currie. We won 3-1 and I was hooked.

A GREEN AND GLORIOUS PITCH
AYRESOME PARK
GLEN DURRANT,
BDO WORLD DARTS CHAMPION 2017 TO 2019

PE Teacher Mr Stewart: "First person to shout out an England Rugby player gets a ticket for the next Boro game."

Glen Durrant: "Peter Winterbottom, Sir."

Class – giggles.

Mr Stewart: "Correct, Durrant."

I arrived with plenty of time before meeting the teacher and the other winners. I looked through the fence to see the finest grass/ pitch I'd ever seen. It was wet and the dew was incredible. I was brimming with excitement. "Award winning pitch that, Durrant," said Mr Stewart. Unfortunately, the tale dies a death, as I don't remember the game apart from the fact Stephen Bell played. All I wanted was his autograph. I have researched each home game 1982/83 and 1983/84 but nothing reminds me of the match that was my first. My sole memory was the pitch. Green and glorious.

BORO 4 – 1 OXFORD UNITED
AYRESOME PARK, MAY 16TH 1967
GORDON COX

The official attendance was 39,683, there is every chance there was a few more, and I was one of them. May 16th 1967 was the first time as a small boy I had ever set foot in Ayresome Park and I was hooked.

A hat trick from John O'Rourke and one from (Sir) John Hickton saw Boro blast past an Oxford United side captained by Ron Atkinson who would go on to achieve so much in the game, and win promotion after just one season in Division 3.

Division what? What had I witnessed? I didn't understand what was going on, many will doubtless argue that nothing has changed. But that night I knew I loved enough of what I had been part of, floodlights, noise, atmosphere, whatever the ingredients, to want more.

Like thousands who started their Boro-supporting journey, I had gone with my dad, a Boro fan for decades. Knowing nothing of a closed-season, I would pester him through the summer to take me again, but it wasn't until the end of September that we could afford to go. We were rewarded with a win over Aston Villa, Hickton the scorer (didn't he score in every single game he played? I'm sure he did, you know). The hero to many of my age battered in a hat trick in the next game, a 5-0 thumping of Plymouth. I was off and running.

I wasn't a Holgate Ender, my dad couldn't stand up all game. We had watched the Oxford match from a seat in the upper part of the North Stand. Occasionally we would return there, but the East End seats were more often than not where we would watch from.

By then I had unknowingly agreed to keep up with tradition. Every Saturday night my dad and I would walk to the paper shop on Roman Road and wait for the Sports, just like hundreds more across the town. It was the only way to find the scores and look at league tables I now understood. It was the same shop that less than a handful of years later would sell me the SHOOT! magazine with league ladders (tables) you changed yourself.

Ayresome became a second, maybe a first, home. It's where I learned about football, about people, about society and where places were in England, and also about Bovril or was it Oxo?

Ayresome Park was where I grew up.

BORO 1 – 0 MAN CITY
AYRESOME PARK, FA CUP 3RD ROUND REPLAY, 18TH JANUARY 1972
GORDON REES

My dad, who was a massive Boro fan, told me I asked to go to the Boro games with him but he thought I was too young. I can still remember reading my dad's Northern Echo the day after we drew 2-2 away to York in a League Cup match, September 1971. I was a month short of 11 years old.

Later on in 71 he took me and my younger brother to a league game. I asked him numerous times who it was against and he couldn't recall. The following January we played 1st Division giants, Man City in the 3rd Round of the FA Cup. I remember watching BBC Grandstand and leading 1-0, then the tickertape at the foot of the screen came up 'Man City 1 Boro 1.'

With 11 minutes remaining underdogs Boro were going to pull off a massive cup shock and win at giants Man City but Franny Lee had other ideas, he threw himself to the ground and won a penalty, which he converted, for a replay at Ayresome Park.

Little did I know that my dad had told our mam that he was going to take both my brother and I to the replay. So, on the snowy Tuesday evening, on January 18th 1972, we set off from West Lane for the short walk to Ayresome Park.

My dad paid me and my brother into the Boys End, a tanner I think [Editor – a tanner was sixpence or 6d, half a shilling or half a bob, it became a 2 1/2p coin in new money], telling us to go to the top of the steps and he will be stood in front of the wall, which separated the Boys End from the Bob End. This would be our spot each week thereafter, against the wall dead centre in the Boys End.

It has been mentioned that star-crazed kids talk about the lush green grass and bright lights and that's exactly what you instantly think of. Also matches were constantly lit in the stands when people were lighting up cigarettes, it was awesome.

I remember Nobby Stiles running out with a brown ball and the roar of the crowd. Nobby looked funny running out with his hair receding. I always thought he ran out of the tunnel looking up to the skies. I don't remember much at all about the game other than Hickton scored at the opposite end, the snow brushed up against the advertising boards and Man City's iconic away strip, still one of my favourite all time away strips to this day. Another thing that still stands out, and as I think back looks in slow motion, Franny Lee must have been getting frustrated and close to the Chicken Run when, Stuey Boam towering above him, sort of picked him up him and moved him away, funny.

Boro won the game 1-0 with a crowd of 39,917, both my brother and I were hooked and from that moment, we stood in that same spot in the Boys End, with our dad in front in the Bob End, magic moments.

When we won the Carling Cup, I travelled down with my dad and when the whistle blew, my brother was sat in front of us, from the Boys End to the Millennium we were together. We had seen everything together and now experienced the pinnacle as a fan. Both are sadly now gone but it is a fantastic ever lasting memory.

LIFE'S HARD WHEN YOU'RE SEVEN
AYRESOME PARK
GORDON STEEL

I was barely seven years old when my dad gave me the most devastating news I had ever had. News that would ultimately change my life forever! Life's hard when you're seven, isn't it? My dad was a welder down Smiths Dock on the banks of the River Tees and although I don't think he ever said it, I knew he loved me, and that's why I was so shocked when he said, "Okay son, you're old enough now. I am going to break your bloody heart."

'Break my heart!' I thought 'Bloody hell.'

I wasn't sure what it meant but it sounded like it would hurt.

"What… wha… what are you going do to me, dad?"

"You are going to become a Middlesbrough supporter. I'm gonna take you to the match."

"And will that break my heart, dad?"

"Oh yes, son – regularly. And they'll keep breaking it for as long as you bloody live."

And so, he took me and our kid to our first ever game: a night match.

He took us to the Boys End, gave us a tanner each to get in and arranged to meet us after the game at the post box on the corner of Clive Road. The Boys End was its own little enclosure for, as the name suggests, boys only. Once through the turnstile I stepped into a dream: a dream that I have been living ever since. Huge lights beamed down on to the greenest grass I'd ever seen. I'd never seen this many grown up people in one place before. At that time we were in the second division and the football couldn't exactly be described as sexy. I don't think it could be described as football. It was a man's game. It was a working man's game. Pre-show hospitality was eating a Newboulds pork pie while paddling in pee as you p*ssed against an outside wall in the pouring rain. And if the players were kicked, they got up, if nothing else to prove it didn't hurt. If they scored a goal, they shook hands. If they scored a hugely important goal, they might do a little skip, a jump and punch the air. Not too high, mind. Overt displays of emotion were definitely frowned upon. And like all good drugs, my first fix got me hooked.

WEST HAM V BORO
GRAHAM GABRIEL

I remember you interviewing me for the Fly Me To The Moon Millannual when I told you about going to a Boro v Leeds Bill Gates Testimonial in May 1974. It turns out that wasn't my first match at all.

Since having that chat with you I've spoken to family who have told me that I was first taken to a match by my dad's uncle when I was about five years old. We'd gone on holiday as a family to London. We had family out Plaistow way, and my dad's uncle worked for Ford in Dagenham. He'd worked there pretty much all his adult life, having left Teesside soon after leaving school. It transpired that while we were there West Ham were hosting Boro and he suggested he take me along. My dad had no interest with football and was happy to babysit my younger brother, while their respective wives went out. So my great uncle took me to The Boleyn Ground, having lived down there so long he was now a full on Hammers fan.

I can't say I have any actual memory of going to the match, or watching it, but a relative told me my great uncle got me to the ground, met up with his West Ham mates and blew them all out to take me into the Boro end, telling them he couldn't have me growing up a Hammers fan in Boro, it just wouldn't sit right. It was Boro he supported, West Ham were just local. I believe, though I've never looked it up, Boro won. It would have been 1970 if you want to check. Around Christmas, as that's when we went on holiday.

I have no clear memories of that day, but many years later, when I was working in the West End, my boss and his wife were Hammers Season Ticket holders, so I would always go along with him, on her ticket, to Boro games.

I found West Ham fans generally very friendly, especially if I told them that story of how close I'd come to being a Hammers fan.

[Editor – the mystery continues because Boro did play West Ham in 1970 but it was an FA Cup tie at Ayresome Park, January 3rd 1970, Boro 2-1 West Ham United.

Interviewed in 2000 Graham said of the testimonial match: I was only nine years old. I went in the Bob End with my friend's dad. Everyone lifted up off their seats when Boro scored. I just remember catching flashes of green between bodies.]

BORO V PRESTON NORTH END
AYRESOME PARK
GRAHAM WRIGHT

Yes, I remember it well, I went alone, I was in the Boys End and they were playing Preston North End. The Bob End was still an open end and all standing. I got the O bus from Stockton and got off at the blind school. I think the Boro won, with Alan Peacock upfront and Gordon Jones playing. He went to my school years ago. I was ten years old and starting to have freedom of movement.

The next match I went to, I jumped over the wall and ran down to pitch side. What a rebel, eh! I think it cost sixpence to get in and back at school I made a rattle in woodwork class, painted it red and white. When I used it at Ayresome, it broke and the head flew into the crowd and hit some bloke on the back of his head. I ducked down.

I remember getting the Football Special bus back to Stockton. They used to go from Church Row. As we passed the 'Dogs' on the Wilderness someone said, look there's Gibbo going for a bet, he must have skipped the bath. Ian Gibson was an inside forward and a crowd favourite, sometimes… lol.

BORO V MAN CITY
AYRESOME PARK, FA CUP REPLAY
HARRY GALLAGHER

My first Boro game was an FA Cup replay against Man City sometime around the turn of the 70s. It was an evening match, so a replay. I was about seven years old. I think we were in the South Stand but can't be sure. My cousin, older than me by ten years, had taken me after much pleading, and it was absolutely packed. I remember the thrill of the Bovril against the evening's cold air but then it all went a bit pear-shaped!

The crowd (all standing obviously) started surging back and forth and it got more and more frantic. I remember at one stage taking my feet off the floor and being carried back and forth by it all. Next thing I knew, I was on the floor with blokes trying to avoid trampling me. Someone must have picked me up and I heard somebody shout, "Get this little lad carried out to the back!" I was passed over heads and deposited at the rear, only to be escorted out with my highly disgruntled cousin being told off for bringing me! He sulked all the way home on the bus! Sad way to remember my first match but there we are! The other thing was who played for them. I remember really wanting to see Colin Bell but not sure he played that night – pretty sure Mike Summerbee did.

[Editor – Most likely this is January 30th 1972 3rd Round replay and Boro won 1-0 through John Hickton defeating a Man City team including Mike Summerbee and Francis Lee and yes, Colin Bell, too – all England internationals.]

BORO 0 – 2 IPSWICH TOWN
AYRESOME PARK, SATURDAY AUGUST 19TH 1967
HARRY GLASPER

I was a sixteen-year-old pupil at Acklam Hall Grammar School when my dad, Ernest Glasper died, aged just 47 in late March 1963. I must confess at this time in my life, cricket was the game I followed because it was a summer sport I played at school. I hated rugby because I was thrust into the heart of the scrum as a nervous hooker. As a six-stone, five feet five sapling I hated being pursued by several sixteen stone opponents, intent on wiping me off the face of the earth.

Sometime after dad's death, mam asked me if I wanted dad's 'stuff' on Middlesbrough FC. The 'stuff' referred to was a few pre-war and post-war programmes and two pocket notebooks. Little did I realise how much the 'stuff' would change my later life.

Christine, my fiancée, worked as an auxiliary nurse and was working on World Cup Final Day in July 1966 so what did I do on that Saturday afternoon? Did I join the rest of England and watch the match live on the telly? No, I chose to go the Odeon cinema. All these years later I cannot remember the film I saw that sunny Saturday afternoon but I do remember coming out of the cinema to be told by a jubilant fan that England won the World Cup.

I was persuaded by Christine and her mother to go to Ayresome Park to watch Boro play against Ipswich Town on Saturday August 19th 1967, in our first game following promotion back into Division Two. We stood in the East End and I do remember the announcement over the PA system saying that Don Masson had married on the morning of the game, some wag stood near me shouted, "What the **** is he doing here on his wedding day?" causing great laughter all around us. The team was announced as the two sides walked onto the pitch in front of a 25,916 crowd. The crowd knew already that Arthur Horsfield would not be playing because he had broken a toe on the first day of pre-season training but then manager Stan Anderson had to draft in local lad Des McPartland as regular keeper Willie Whigham had injured his hip in a Hutton Road training session.

Ayresome Park continued to be a lucky ground for Ipswich Town as they recorded their fourth win in eight League visits with a 0-2 win. Boro centre-half Dicky Rooks failed to clear a 21st minute cross to Ray Crawford, and with keeper Des McPartland out of position, Ray body-swerved past him and put the ball into the empty net. Ten minutes into the second half Town went further ahead – Danny Hegan sent Bill Baker away, and he evaded the attentions of Boro skipper Gordon Jones to make it 0-2. Boro's casualties were Don Masson (twisted ankle) and Derrick Downing (groin strain) and both missed the following Tuesday's 4-1 League Cup victory over Barnsley at Ayresome Park.

By the time November 30th 1968 came around, I was fervently committed to the Boro cause as much as the staunchest supporters of many years standing. Christine and myself had married at Grange Road Registry Office on the morning of this game and after a small wedding reception we walked the short distance from Beadon Grove, West Lane to Ayresome Park. The circumstances were different to the Ipswich Town game – thankfully, there was no PA announcement of our wedding and Boro beat Blackburn Rovers 2-0 with a John Coddington own goal on 37 minutes and Derrick Downing in the final minute of the game.

BORO 9 – 0 BRIGHTON
AYRESOME PARK, AUGUST 23RD 1958
HARRY GREENMON

My first Boro game was the first game of the 1958/59 season. Home to Brighton. I was ten years old at the time. We won 9-0. No wonder I was hooked for life. Clough scored 5, Peacock 2 and Bill Harris scored a couple of penalties. We lived in Thorntree and if my memory is correct we travelled to town on the Y bus. I went with my father. I remember we got to the ground quite early and dad took me to the Boys End turnstiles, paid for me to get in and told me to go to the front left corner of the enclosure where he would meet me. I did and when we met up, he lifted me over the wall and we went down to the front and we watched the match from there.

I remember thinking how fantastic the pitch looked. It was the first game of the season so it was in the best condition it could be. I can't remember too much about the game itself apart from the score although I remember how quickly it passed. It looked like we could score every time we attacked. Brighton were lucky it was only 9. Like I said, after that performance I was hooked for life.

BORO 4 – 0 CARLISLE UNITED
AYRESOME PARK, DECEMBER 23RD 1967
HARRY PEARSON

I was six years old and it was it was two days before Christmas. I'm not sure how I persuaded my parents it was a good idea, by pestering all week most likely, but eventually they agreed to let me go to Ayresome Park. My grandad was supposed to drive over and pick me up, but for some reason he went on ahead and my Uncle Les, back from college for the holidays, turned up instead. My Uncle Les drank cups of tea, ate sandwiches and chatted with my mum and dad. Time wound on. We set off and got snarled up in traffic, creeping past the Southern Cross Hotel, Marton shops and Bertram Ramsay School. Eventually my uncle gave up and parked somewhere near Clairville Stadium. He was 21, with no experience of children. What was to him a brisk 15 minute walk was a marathon for an infant school kid. We got to Ayresome at 2.45. Uncle Les had arranged to meet my grandad in the Bob End seats, but neither of them had factored in the attractions of the mighty Cumbrians. For the previous home game – v Crystal Palace – just over 16,000 had attended, but today there was close to 28,000 in the ground. The Bob End was full. So was the South Stand. The only place where the turnstiles weren't shut was the Holgate. We struggled into the south-west corner just after kick off.

A packed Holgate filled with festive cheer was not a good place for a six-year old to watch football. I could barely glimpse the pitch. My uncle let me sit on his shoulders until his back gave out. I have a vague memory of watching John O'Rourke strike a shot from near the penalty spot into the Holgate End goal, but I may have imagined it. O'Rourke did get a hat trick that afternoon and Boro won 4-0.

But we'd left long before the end, my uncle eager to avoid the rush and put an end to my ceaseless complaining that my hands were cold, I couldn't see and my legs ached from all the standing. He's never been to football with me since.

BORO 0 – 1 WEST HAM
AYRESOME PARK, 1990
HELEN SCOTT

My first match was slightly later than my sister Lou's and actually a bit of a story. It was West Ham early 1990. It was that odd game that they decided if you had a ticket stub for it, you would get priority for Wembley tickets for the ZDS cup final. So we got up at some ungodly hour, went and queued round by the cemetery for five hours and got our West Ham tickets. We stood in the Holgate End and I remember I'd never experienced anything like it, the ground was packed for a fairly meaningless league game. We lost 0-1. I remember there being quite a lot of grumbling fans and at one point a man shouted so loud, I was pretty scared! I turned round to realise that the very loud man was in fact my dad who I really had never heard shout like that before. But the result didn't matter because we were going to Wembley! Except I didn't get to go – shortly afterwards my dad had his car accident and we ended up visiting him in hospital that afternoon. I could have gone, we got the tickets – drove up to the ticket office and bought them with no queue at all! But it didn't seem right. Lou and my auntie had Season Tickets by then and so the next season I got one as well. And that was the start of that!

BORO 2 – 1 PLYMOUTH ARGYLE
AYRESOME PARK, APRIL 1992
HENRY CARDEN

My first Boro match was back in April 1992 for a hard-fought 2-1 victory over Plymouth Argyle at Ayresome Park. I remember being totally in awe of the crowd and the noise. That buzz you feel when you see all of the fans approaching the ground never goes, does it? Most of all though, sadly, I remember getting food poisoning from a burger. If I recall correctly, that was the main catalyst in becoming a vegetarian. Or was it that gruesome documentary about battery farmed hens? Either way, unfortunately the memory of the incessant spewing has all but eclipsed the hazy recollection of Willie Falconer smashing the winner into the top corner from just off the left-wing against pompous right-winger Peter Shilton in the Argyle goal.

BORO V TORQUAY UNITED
AYRESOME PARK, APRIL 29TH 1967
HEREWARD KAYE (FORMERLY OF THE FLYING PICKETS)

Playing football in the garden of our house in Orchard Road, Linthorpe, a ghostly roar would float across the ether. Before I was old enough to know or passionately care, it was unsettling, other worldly. It was the voice of multitudes in acclaim, faintly heard, but as it passed overhead it left one in no doubt that something miraculous had happened. And it had – Boro had scored a goal!

Ayresome Park was a mile up the road and I remember, when I had a few more years on the clock, walking to the ground on match-day for the first time. I had my school-friend Titch Wright in tow. He wasn't even a Boro fan – whereas I was a fully paid-up Ayresome Angel. But he came along. We were both thirteen – and we were heading for the Holgate End, the first time I was allowed to venture into the lions den, unaccompanied by an adult.

As I marched along to an ever-quickening beat, the match-day momentum billowed up all around me, often on alcoholic fumes, as from pubs and bars spilled Boro fans, all in red and white scarves, some with rattles. That was me, plus a klaxon and a tin hat. All would undoubtedly be confiscated these days. I wore a long white overall from my dad's shop Kayes Tools, splashed with crimson-painted names of all my heroes that season: Whigham, Hickton, O'Rourke, 'King' Arthur (that was Arthur Horsfield, who sneaked over to send me and my mate Alistair Powell to the shop for a packet of fags once, when we were watching training).

Roman Road, Devonshire, Chipchase, the crowd begins to bottleneck. Then we're at the Holgate End, being sucked through the turnstiles and in. It hits you all at once as a child, the vista opening out – the vivid green of the pitch, the main stand looking as long as the Dorman Long building along the Trunk Road, the clamour, the expectation. That first time standing in the Kop, it was a little frightening too, which only heightened the thrill.

The sides emerge to a full-throttled roar and here are my heroes in the flesh, heading imaginary crosses, powering in invisible volleys.

Titch and I are standing about four rows up from the goal, just left of the stanchion, as Willy Whigham drops his gloves in the corner and gets a feel of his space. You saw them all taking up their position, you knew them all so well: Dickie Rooks, stocky, curly, all blond bonhomie, about to boss it at centre-half. Geoff Butler trotting back into the left back position. "Butler for England! Butler for England!" comes the throaty cry from behind my head. Manager Stan Anderson takes his place in the dug-out and Harold Shepherdson, Mr 'magic-sponge', roams the touchline in a blue track-suit.

Gordon Jones loses the toss and both sides turn around. Boro would be attacking the Holgate End, which meant those distant, remote forwards I worshipped would be piling in towards us, any minute now. The ref's looking at his watch, whistle in mouth. The police are keeping a glad-eye out. It isn't quite time for 'we'll hang the referee from the stands' and 'who's that copper jumpin over the wall? Dixon, Dixon…' but it's coming and the game's underway.

Prolific strike partners (yes, there used to be such a thing at Middlesbrough!) Hickton and O'Rourke power towards us, fed from left and right by wingers Dave Chadwick and Derrick Downing. Hickton unleashes a thunderbolt that just shaves the left-hand post.

"Wow, Titch, see that?"

Sadly, no, or he might have got out the way. As it was, my vertically-challenged friend was head-height to the ball when it struck him full in the mush. Now he was laid out on the concrete. I turned to Titch and Hickton turned to follow the game upfield – but on three occasions he returned and each time planted the ball in the back of the net. John O'Rourke got another and the roar that I had grown up with as a child, ghostly and ethereal from a mile away was a joyful, deafening tumult all around me now and my voice was part of the orchestra.

I sang all the way home too – though Titch was strangely subdued.

BORO 4 – 4 LEEDS
AYRESOME PARK, BILL GATES TESTIMONIAL, MAY 1974
IAN HARRIS

Although I am told Boro v Sheffield Wednesday was my first game, I have little recollection of this despite the 8-0 victory. The first game I do remember vividly was the Boro v Leeds Bill Gates testimonial match in May 1974. I had just turned six a couple of weeks before and I remember being taken to the game by my dad. We travelled in two cars with my brothers, uncles and cousins. I am not sure how we all managed to fit in as, from memory, there was at least twelve of us! It was the only game I can remember going to with my dad before he died.

The traffic from Billingham to Middlesbrough was really busy. It was before the flyover was built and I can remember sitting in traffic jams over Newport Bridge and all the way to Ayresome Park. We parked up and walked in a big crowd to the turnstiles. I was sitting on my dad's shoulders and getting passed from one to another until we arrived. We watched from the open corner in the Holgate End, next to the North Stand. Both teams did a lap of honour with trophies before the match started. The ground was packed and noisy. I have memories of sitting on the barriers and also running down to the toilet to find it was just a brick wall!

The game finished in a 4-4 draw and I can remember seeing Alan Foggon scoring, in fact I think he got a hat trick but I can't really remember who scored the other Boro goal. I think Peter Lorimer scored one of the Leeds goals and I seem to think that the Leeds goalie, David Harvey, got stretchered off at some point during the match. I had never been somewhere with that many people, so much noise and excitement. The seed was sown and it's been in my blood ever since. If only every match could be like that first one.

A SCARY EXPERIENCE AS A CHILD
AYRESOME PARK
IAN RICHARDSON

This is so hard, because I vaguely remember my dad taking me to Ayresome Park as a child to see a game of which I can't remember unfortunately. I think I must have been about five years old or so. I was cold, I couldn't see a thing for the crowds of people all stood up. All I could see were the pockets on the jackets. I think I had a pocket full of sweets. The noise was deafening, I remember and I got quite scared by the loud singing and yelling. I remember my dad lifting me up, we must have scored, I didn't know what was happening, but I knew everyone was cheering around me.

I'm sorry I can't remember the team we played, to be honest it was a scary experience as a child. What a weakling. I only wish I had pursued going to see the Boro. Although as I grew older I always followed the teams but only started going to the Riverside for the odd games. I decided to get myself a Season Ticket because deep inside I knew I wanted to. It was the child inside telling me to do it, and I am so glad I did. I love match days. The breakfast on Saturday mornings, the beers before the match, the free pint at the ground, the atmosphere of the Riverside crowd and the regulars who sit around me. It's become a family ritual on Saturdays and on evening games.

BORO 6 – 0 LEICESTER CITY
AYRESOME PARK, SEPTEMBER 29TH 1990
IAN SMITH

My first game memories are from the 1990/91 season and a home game against Leicester City, and you may remember that game ended 6-0 to the Boro! However, it's been a source of gentle disagreement amongst the family as my dad claims I had already been to a game before that, but can't remember which one! So given my first memories are of this game, my mind always heads to it as the first I attended when anyone asks (I'm still not convinced that I went any earlier, despite my dad's protestations).

I can only assume I was reliably informed by my dad that day that it wasn't always like that following the Boro. Emphatic results, hammering sides is the exception not the rule, yet in a strange kind of way I like it like that, makes you appreciate it all the more when those exceptions come around. My positivity knows no bounds, it seems.

Outside of the game itself, my recollections are sadly lacking, though I can only surmise that we ended up at the chippy on Essex Street near Ayresome Park prior to the match. We would more often than not pay a pre-match to visit the establishment run by Steve Gibson's uncle. The mere fact he was a relation to the Boro owner added a sprinkle of glamour to what is essentially a modest, albeit tasty, takeaway. It showed just how much of an impact Gibson had on fans, that six-year-old me would be more than intrigued at having his battered sausage and chips handed to him by the uncle of the messiah.

Though it was before the days of all the family having a Season Ticket (that would come the following year), we will have taken our seats in the North Stand Upper. I always loved that vantage point, and whilst I looked on enviously at times at the atmosphere in the Holgate End, I always preferred the idea of sitting, being able to study the game. Just looking back now, entering through those famous gates and milling around before kick-off waiting for players to arrive, it brings back a huge rush of nostalgia. Heading up the steps, looking out on to the pitch, a beautiful sea of green – I would always imagine running out on to the hallowed turf, an experience I was luckily able to have when I was mascot a few years later.

Anyway, as for the game itself, being just six at the time makes it nigh on impossible for me to remember anything beyond the obvious, not that the obvious isn't absolute gold for the nostalgic soul in me. If it's not the heavy involvement John Hendrie had in the game, firing home one at the keeper's near post, and assisting a couple more, it's the artistry in Bernie Slaven's goal. Hooking it back over his head and swivelling, he manages to complete this one single movement with a looping strike into the keeper's top corner. One of my first tastes of Bernie's genius, in the flesh at least – I'd already been introduced heavily to his exploits via the many highlights my dad had shown me, as well as the 1988/89 season review on VHS that I'd go on to wear out over the ensuing years (that hat trick against Coventry away lives long in the memory).

The other strikes from Jimmy Phillips, Ian Baird and a Paul Kerr double strangely aren't as easy to recollect, and required a YouTube visit to reacquaint myself with them. Likely down to my obsession with the other two scorers on the day no doubt.

I'll continue to believe that thrashing of The Foxes was my first taste of live Boro action, but maybe it wasn't and it was more like a glum 0-0 on a rainy midweek outing? It might just be my memory being selective, but as selective memories go, it sure isn't a bad one.

BORO 3 – 0 NOTTS COUNTY
AYRESOME PARK, AUGUST 20TH 1955
MIKE SMITH

From my dad's memories (they were sketchy in parts, I did some research) , it was the 1955/56 season and as far as I can remember it was the first game in August against Notts County.

I remember my dad sitting me on the wall at the back (North East corner). As my dad was tall, he always stood right at the back. I also remember being frightened by the noise; I had never been anywhere where there were big crowds.

We won the game (the final score was 3-0, two goals from Arthur Fitzsimons and another from Lindy Delapenha), and I also remember well the journey to the game.

We got the bus from Berwick Hills to Middlesbrough Town Centre near the Town Hall, walking from there to Ayresome Park. I was only eight-years-old and I remember saying, "My legs are tired, Dad," and about half way up Linthorpe Road he put me on his shoulders. It was a long walk from the town to Ayresome Park!

BORO 1 – 0 WEST BROMICH ALBION
AYRESOME PARK, OCTOBER 23RD 1976
IAN WILSON

My first game was against West Brom in October 1976 as a seven year old. David Mills scored the winner to put us top of the First Division. In fact, going top and it being announced by Bernard Gent at the end of the game is the thing that stands out for me in my memory. It's also the only time we've 'properly' been top flight league leaders in my 45 years of supporting the Boro (I discount alphabetical order and after only one or two games... which I seem to recall may have happened late 90s?!).

I remember the lead up to the game having pestered my old fella (a veteran of Cloughie and Peacock days) to take me after watching us on Shoot a few weeks before. I must have just started getting into football that season as the first game I can remember watching properly on TV was the 1976 Cup Final (Southampton beating Man Utd). We sat in the East End Seats and I think my dad might even have 'lifted' me over the turnstile... he said that's what everyone did (no wonder our crowds in the 70s seemed lower than they looked!). As others have said before, the first thing that struck you about Ayresome Park on first sight was how green and big the pitch was.

My other main memory was that Johnny Giles was player manager for the Baggies, something that seemed very unusual to me then and after. I guess today his Leeds connection with Big Jack would be hyped up to death.

I was hooked after this game and remember a fairly exciting season, challenging for Europe and reaching the sixth round of the FA Cup which then fizzled out (typical Boro in the late 70s!).

BORO 1 – 1 WIMBLEDON
AYRESOME PARK, LEAGUE CUP, OCTOBER 25TH 1989
J.P. RIGGALL

Well, I've got two memories really. I remember a game that was in the League Cup v Wimbledon, October 25th 1989. We drew 1 each. I remember it mainly because there was a low attendance and I spent my time running up and down the aisle from my seat right at the top in the North Stand Upper.

I started to really get into football shortly after that and had a Season Ticket which was North lower, left of the dug out. I sometimes sat just right of the dugout as my brother was a YTS and got two tickets for each game.

My first big memory was beating Newcastle

4-1 on the last day of the season. After that I was really into kits so would try and remember the team we were playing and draw it when I got home, particularly the rancid West Brom yellow and green kit with the squared pattern shorts.

BORO 0 – 1 CRYSTAL PALACE
AYRESOME PARK, DECEMBER 28TH 1992
JANET HAIGH CLARKE

My first game was against Crystal Palace on a Tuesday night. My auntie won tickets in a raffle and I went with my sister (Anna). We sat in the East Stand and the pitch was incredibly green under the floodlights. I remember sitting near a pack of scouts, Tommy Wright playing and Jamie Pollock being subbed. I thought we won, but having just checked we lost 1 nil!

Jamie Haigh Clarke's first game was Wednesday away. He wore the yellow away strip and Jamie couldn't get over the crowd and the noise. He was three (August 29th 2015, Sheffield Wednesday 1-3 Middlesbrough).

PRE-SEASON FRIENDLY
RIVERSIDE STADIUM, 1996
JAYNE HALEY

Myself, my brother and sister all have the same memory of our first game. It was 1996. Until this point the Riverside was somewhere my dad went but we were told we weren't old enough. It was a night match, I think a pre-season friendly, I'm not sure who against. Dad brought three t-shirts home with him for us to wear from the club shop in the Cleveland Centre. Blue t-shirts with a little white feather on the left top pocket area and Ravanelli 11 on the back. The excitement of going was what we remember more than the game. The only memory I have of the game was a man sat behind us shouting "Butch dingle" every time Phil Stamp got the ball.

There is nothing more exciting than walking to such a huge place as a child and seeing so many people walking towards the stadium and then hearing the crowd. Those are the days we are waiting to come back.

BORO 2 – 3 BURY
AYRESOME PARK, APRIL 12TH 1969
JILL ATKINSON

You might have thought naming your first Boro game was quite an easy task, but for me it's quite tricky. Mind you, I have really enjoyed looking into it.

I have never known the identity of my first game for certain. I have put together all the clues and memories I have and may have come up with an answer. It could possibly have been Boro v Bury on April 12th 1969.

I know the game was not long before I went to Secondary School, and that was in September 1969.

I know we were in the Second Division. I know Willie Whigham was in goal because I thought he had a funny name. I think McMordie scored because I remember my dad telling me Eric was a friend of George Best. I know it wasn't mid-winter because we came home in daylight. However, during my research, I have discovered that the Government experimented that year with no Greenwich Meantime and we did not put the clocks back in October 1968 or forward in March 1969, so it may have been daylight at 5pm earlier in 1969. I know we lost (2-3).

In the first half my dad sat me on the wall. We were in the corner, the Clive Road End, and in the second half I kicked my Bovril cup around, up and down the steps of the terracing. I don't think I was too interested in the game really. How things have changed! There can't have been many people there if I had room to have a kick about. I have looked up the attendance for that game and it was just 10,417.

I know my dad and I travelled to Ayresome Park by car and we used to park in the streets behind the Swedish Mission Church and walk across Linthorpe Road by St Barnabas Church to get to Ayresome Park.

Although I'll never be sure, you are welcome to use the Boro v Bury game as my first Boro match.

BORO 1 – 0 BLACKPOOL
AYRESOME PARK, OCTOBER 1971
JIM PLATT, FORMER BORO PLAYER

It was a massive step for me to come over to England as an eighteen year old. As everyone knows, I was homesick and didn't perform to the best of my ability. Luck plays a huge part in players' careers and with Willie Whigham having a poor game against Sunderland (4-1) I think Stan Anderson was probably forced to make a change. People were telling me I would be playing on Saturday. Sunderland was midweek. Willie was at fault for two goals. My debut was against Blackpool at home. I think I only knew when the team sheet went up on Friday. We won 1-0 so a clean sheet was welcome. I don't remember much about it except that the older players were very supportive – as was Stan. John Burridge was in goal for Blackpool and he wished me the best of luck before the match.

Years later (Boro's cup winning coach) Steve Harrison told me he was making his debut for Blackpool that day too.

BORO 1 – 2 HULL CITY
AYRESOME PARK, FEBRUARY 5TH 1955
JIMMY FLYNN

I thought my first Boro game at Ayresome
Park was Boro v Hull City in 1956, the game
in which Wilf Mannion came back to Boro for
the Tigers. I now realise this was a mistake. My
first game was indeed Boro v Hull City and
it was Wilf's first return to Ayresome Park in
the colours of another club, but the date was
February 5th 1955.

I was aged eight and was accompanied to
the game by my cousin David Heaney and my
future brother in law, Joe McCabe both aged
twelve. We walked from my cousin's home
on Grange Road, along Southfield Road, up
Linthorpe Road, down Ayresome Street and
we watched the game from the Boys End
enclosure.

My main recollection of the game is of the
blond haired, mystic Mannion, the noise of
the crowd and the vivid colours of the green
pitch and orange ball and the players' shirts,
the gold and black of Hull and the vivid red
of Boro. It seemed a wondrous place with a

strange aroma, which I now know was the mix of tobacco smoke, meat pies and Bovril which only existed in football stadia. Throughout my childhood, my father had regaled me and my two brothers with tales of Wilf. So, this was a wonderful memory from far away and long ago. UTB.

MAN UNITED 3 – 1 BORO
OLD TRAFFORD, FA CUP, JANUARY 3RD 1999
JOE HAMMILL, CATTLE AND CANE

My first was Boro v Man United in the FA Cup. Andy Townsend put us 1-0 up. It was a false dawn. We lost 3-1. Nicky Butt dived for a penalty. Disgrace

I remember I went with my older brother James and his best mate Pinkey. We travelled in Pinkey's new mini. Loved the atmosphere.

BORO 1 – 1 WIGAN
RIVERSIDE STADIUM, DECEMBER 9TH 2006
JOE NICHOLSON

The first football match I went to was on my tenth birthday when Gareth Southgate's Middlesbrough side played Wigan at the Riverside on December 9th 2006. My parents weren't massive football fans but I'd really gotten into Boro's UEFA Cup run so just wanted to go to a match. The game finished 1-1, with Yakubu equalising in the second half after Henri Camara had opened the scoring from the penalty spot. I remember the excitement walking to the ground, seeing players like Mark Viduka and Stewart Downing who I'd watched on TV. My mum also got a birthday message to appear on the scoreboard before the match. I loved the atmosphere as the floodlights came on in the second half, cheering when Boro scored and staying until the end to clap the players off. I've been going back ever since.

WE'RE GOING TO THE MATCH, ME AND YOU
AYRESOME PARK, 1957
JOHN CULLY

I was only five, my Boro home debut on a big green double-decker 'match special' from Doggy market place. Off at the cenotaph, down Kensington Road we quickened our pace.

"Stay close to me, we'll get a squeeze into the Bob End." We marched with ease up those concrete steps without a hitch, my first ever view of that marvellous pitch, that grass so green it seemed to glow. Short-sleeved red shirts, white v-necks, far down below.

Then the most amazing sight of all. A giant West Indian man, he looked seven foot tall shouting, "Come on Boro, Give Our Kid the ball!"

I looked up in awe, he had the crowd in delirium. His name was Astor, the North East's only black comedian.

Didn't see the match, I just watched Astor, comedian and singer. 'Our kid' was Lindy Delapenha, Boro's Jamaican winger.

Astor's booming voice was so loud I couldn't comprehend, when he shouted they laughed at the opposite side of the ground in the Holgate End.

BORO 0 – 1 LIVERPOOL
AYRESOME PARK, MAY 11TH 1979
JOHN FOSTER

May 11th 1979, it was an evening game against the all conquering, top-of-the-table Liverpool with Graeme Souness now part of the Anfield ranks. I was nearly seven years of age and dad thought this might be a more 'happier' game to go to, as we remember, the late 70s wasn't exactly a family friendly football time. He was a policeman and had worked plenty of matches so had seen a few things in his time.

I went with my dad and sister, Julie, on the Cleveland Transit No 1 Saltersgill circular from our home in Beechwood. Getting off in Linthorpe Village and making the Clive Road walk to the ground, I remember seeing more and more people converging on Ayresome Park and wondering would the atmosphere get to me too? I'd been a football fan for a couple of years now but this was the first time I would see a live game. The air was punctuated with the smell of burgers, onions and Bovril too. Clusters of people dotted about, no doubt deep in conversation about tonight's game, last weekend's night out at The Madhouse or The Kirk, the new female Prime Minister (who had come to power the week before) or seeing 'Chubby' Brown at The Ladle recently. All were heading towards the floodlights, which were on, guiding our approach and landing into Ayresome Park.

We were going to be in the northeast family enclosure. As we climbed the huge concrete steps in the stand, I remember looking up and seeing the light getting brighter and brighter until, there it was this huge expanse of green – lush, flat green that seemed to go on forever under those enormous floodlights that picked out every detail. In, what seemed to be the far distance, was the Holgate with Middlesbrough General behind it.

The players were already warming up with Liverpool in front of us. Ray Clemence, Kenny

Dalglish, David Johnson, Alan Hansen, Jimmy Case, Alan and Ray Kennedy, Phil Thompson, Terry McDermott, Phil Neal and Graeme Souness were the starting line up in their white Umbro shirts and black shorts.

Boro were up the far end but I noticed David Armstrong, Bosco Jankovic straight away and Jim Platt in goal. Stuart Boam still had his shop and I remember going in there and marvelling that here was Boro's captain selling me some sherbet dip-dabs! Others in the lineup show you just what a great Boro side that was and should've gone on to greater things. John Craggs, Tony McAndrew, Ian Bailey, Mark Proctor, John Mahoney, Billy Ashcroft and David Hodgson.

I do remember the family enclosure to be quite sparsely populated and having a whole crash barrier to sit on. The legendary voice of Bernard Gent was crackling through the tannoy as he played the hits of day, which looking down some old charts for May 1979, Boney M, ABBA, Roxy Music and The Monks – 'Nice legs, shame about the face' (not sure that would've been played on Radio Ayresome). I'm sure he will have welcomed us to 'the happiest place on earth' but I missed that as I devoured every article and advert in the 15p programme! 'ICI Petrol - the straightest deal you can get.' Trying to work out the scoreboard was a bit mind-boggling too. Orange, green or yellow…

No pie or Bovril for us, dad has bought a flask of soup, oxtail if memory serves.

As for the game itself, I don't really remember much detail. I know Liverpool won 0-1 and David Johnson scored. I remember feeling disappointed that it wasn't Kenny Dalglish as everyone raved about him and he can't be that good if he didn't score in every game and of course I was more disappointed that Boro hadn't scored too.

Legendary chants of the day, "You are my Boro," "6ft2, eyes of Blue, Stuey Boam," and "You're going to get your ******* head kicked in," filtered around the ground as I sheepishly thought 'Swear word!!'

32,244 attended the game which shocked me because, as I said, the Family Enclosure and East Stand didn't seem that full!

My other abiding memories are waiting

for the bus to take us home to Beechwood and standing outside the Swedish mission on Linthorpe Road and looking up at the floodlights as their relentless beam shone down and thinking, 'Wow, are they ever going to turn them off?'

Finally, Van McCoy's The Shuffle was being played by Bernard Gent over the tannoy as we left the ground. (No, not the whistley tune!) Whenever I hear that, I always think of Clive Road!

BORO 0 – 0 MILLWALL
AYRESOME PARK, LEAGUE CUP, OCTOBER 1965
JOHN PEACH

Mine was a League Cup game against Millwall in October 1965. I went with a bunch of lads from school, taking the O bus from Norton Green and we went in the Chicken Run. All I really remember was how green the grass looked under the lights and how exciting it looked in the Holgate. Final score was 0-0 and we lost the replay. Typical Boro, but enough to have me hooked and it was always the Holgate after that.

BORO 2 – 0 PEOPLE'S REPUBLIC OF CHINA
AYRESOME PARK, AUGUST 4TH 1979
JOHN WILBERFORCE

My first Boro game wasn't against Sunderland, Newcastle United, Leeds, or Liverpool. Oh no. Not a normal opponent for my first Boro match.

My first game, as a seven-year-old, was on August 4th 1979. And the opponents were none other than the People's Republic of China.

Although I was seven, and born in the Boro, we had actually left Teesside in 1975, and lived in Warrington. We were one of many expat Teesside families in that area, who moved because of the burgeoning chemical plants in Runcorn and Widnes run by ICI. As a consequence, I had spent a couple of years getting into Rugby League – and my first 'real' sporting love was actually Widnes RLFC. We actually had Season Tickets. For me, football at that point was highlights on the TV, and every goal was a long range effort that pinged into the roof of the net – they were goals that the highlights showed, I suppose. Similarly, Rugby League was a very different game – there were tries every ten minutes, and Widnes (at the time) were very good indeed. Indeed, I saw Widnes lift the Challenge Cup at Wembley before I watched the Boro at all.

Anyway, it was a warm Saturday in early August, and we parked on the other side of Warwick Street, in the terraced houses there. And I can remember we stood towards the back of the corner between the North Stand and the East End – we queued up next to the school. Hand on heart, I can't remember much about the game actually. We won 2-0 (in truth, I can't remember the second goal, and we missed the first because I went to the toilet apparently). I can remember the Chinese players being tiny, and being able to hear the players shouting at each other in a language I couldn't understand! After the game, we had chips in the car (a Daf 66, chocolate brown), and went back to my grandma's in Redcar – she lived on Thrush Road above a butcher's shop that she had previously owned with my grandad before he died.

Nowadays, I watch the Boro a lot more than Widnes, although I still look out for their scores. Boro became 'predominant' in my sporting life in around 1984. We never lived on Teesside again, but once I passed my driving test in 1989, I stopped going five times a year, and started going 20-30 times a year, all over the country in my little Nissan Micra.

A love was born.

BORO V NORWICH
WEMBLEY, PLAY OFF FINAL 2015
JUDE, AGED TEN
AS TOLD TO GRANDAD, NEIL WHELDON

As I am now one of the Boro fans who have seen Boro play at Wembley, play in the Premier League and the Championship and have a season messed up half way through, I thought I would tell you all about the first Boro match I went to.

My brother (Ben), grandad and cousin Joe were all Season Ticket holders when the Boro magnificently played their way to the playoff final. I was only five at the time and mam said

I was too young to go to matches. She said no one was allowed to go until they can tie their own Boro scarf and Ben wouldn't show me how to do it.

When we played Brentford in the semi final, Dad said that if we got to Wembley he was going to try and get me, my sister Mia (who was eleven) and Uncle David (who probably had a bit of hair then) and himself tickets to Wembley. The day the tickets went on sale, dad was all prepared with millions of computers and phones trying to get tickets and luckily he did. Not only did he get tickets, they were top of the range (or so grandad said).

We decided to go to London the day before and stay in a hotel. I may have only been five, but I remember the hotel was posh. It was in a place called Watford. It was so posh they even had free coco pops and Nutella. Nobody even cared if you put some Nutella in your sky rocket for later.

We all went to London on Sunday to see if all of the Boro fans were there carrying on. It was amazing. I remember shouting "Come On Boro, Come on Boro" and loads of Boro fans singing it as well. Some daft lads filled the fountain up with washing up liquid, but we didn't see it as I was waffling a pizza in the hotel.

On the day of the match, I remember getting up and going down for coco pops and a sneaky Nutella and seeing loads of Boro fans wearing Boro tops and all looked excited. I managed to sneak four packets of Nutella into my pocket, so I thought it really was the best day ever.

We had to go to Wembley to meet grandad, Joe and Uncle David. We all walked to the train station to get to Wembley and the tube was full of Boro fans. Everyone was carrying on. The lads at the back of the carriage were singing "We're the back end, we're the back end, We're the back end Red Army," then the front end were singing, "we're the front end, we're the front end, we're the front end Red Army." It lasted all the way to Wembley and we laughed like Billi-o.

When we got to Wembley, we met up with grandad and dad bought some drinks and Subway sandwiches for dinner. I remember saying to grandad that the lad who owned Subway was on to a winner with these, but grandad thought they were daft and not as good as Greggs. It was really sunny and I remember thinking that I was glad mam wasn't with us because there were millions of shops and she would have dragged us round them all while she tried everything on.

When it got close to time to go to the match, Uncle David decided he wanted some chips so we queued to get some, only to find out that they cost millions. Uncle David grumbled but bought some anyway. Joe went to have some and spilled a few on the floor. Grandad said that Joe spilt about £4.50 worth and we all laughed.

As we walked into the stadium, everyone I saw told me that the arch across Wembley had a Boro top in it from when it was made. I asked them if they knew whose it was and what the lad now wears to the match but no one knew. My mam would have battered me if I had done that with my top.

When we went into the stadium, it was massive. I remember dad kept tight hold of me and Mia. We found our seats right above the entrances in the corner. Dad hung his scarf over the edge and we were ready to watch the mighty Boro smash Norwich. Then disaster.

Ben put his hand into his bag and realised that mam had forgot to pack the lucky Curly Wurlys. Ben and grandad always had a Curly Wurly at the matches but mam had forgot to pack them. I knew then it wasn't going to be Boro's day.

Ninety minutes is a long time when you are five and dad said I slept through most of the match which was just as well. Me, Ben and dad have now forgiven mam, but every time someone mentions Curly Wurlys, we remember the day.

The weekend was amazing and from then on, I have never gone more than two days without wearing a Boro top. On the way back, we went to Harry Potter Studios. Dad pretended it was my birthday and the Mrs let me open the door to the studio. It was good but I would rather have seen Boro get promoted and one year later I did.

BORO V MAN CITY
AYRESOME PARK, DECEMBER 1976
JULIE ASKINS

I can barely recall my first game – I know it was Man City, at home, and it was a draw. I've just checked the dates and it was December 1976 so I would have been seven. I went with my dad, can't remember if any of my other siblings were there, but I have a feeling my sister might have been there. We sat in the stand opposite the tunnel and although I can't remember anything about the game I can remember my dad going on about Dennis Tueart (bizarre, I know).

BORO V PLYMOUTH
RIVERSIDE STADIUM, 2012/13
KHADIM HUSSAIN

From BELA to Boro to Riverside Ballay! Ballay! For most, their memory of their path to becoming a footballer supporter is the desire to emulate a hero, father, grandfather, uncle or an elder brother who would introduce them to the Saturday afternoon national past time – to watch their local team play. They lucky ones wore their team shirt, beanie and scarf. My introduction was "Khadim, come and read a poem at the launch of my fmttm fanzine?"

"Bob, I have a few Haikus about football but none for Middlesbrough FC!"

He looked at me and said, "You have two weeks, write one!"

Ballay! Ballay! Meri Team Dekho! The first Punjabi poem about Middlesbrough FC and according to my research the only Punjabi poem about football, my root to becoming a football fan at the tender age of 54.

My first match, beginning of the 2012/13 season, the fourth day of Ramadan, I was fasting at the Riverside against Plymouth. After the Seheri (breakfast) before starting Ramadan around 2.30am, a quick prayers and back to alarm set at 12 noon – I'm going to first match. T-shirt with Boro top on top and a warm winter jacket and a Boro scarf, met Andy Willoughby outside at Doc Brown's and walked to the Riverside Stadium. Not much of a crowd, I thought. We did not miss the photo opportunity, in the Boro, the Ayresome gates and of course with statue of the Boro legend Wilf Mannion. The ground seemed almost empty, that was because we were there almost two hours before kick-off. By kick-off the crowd was about 18,000. Some of the Boro crowd were in good voice. The away fans were also in good form as well. On paper we were the weakest team (which improved in the next couple of weeks, thank God). Rain started before kick-off and it rained throughout the match. Compared to our team, the away team seemed like giants. They tried intimidating tactics, but to my delight and all my fellow supporters, we responded in kind. It was a start of the campaign, both teams trying to gel, and the honours were even and we felt a point was gained. It was a game played in a monsoon.

BORO 3 – 0 SPURS
AYRESOME PARK
LAURI COX

I was five and my Uncle Ronnie took me in the stands. I didn't understand the offside rule at that age and asked him why the man kept putting his flag up and he said he had spotted a worm.

I lived on Ayresome Park Road so used to wave to all the fans and police horses from my top window, but I remember having to walk around a different way to get in, we weren't allowed directly in from the end of our street.

The noise and atmosphere was incredible and it had me hooked (mind, I had no chance with dad and Uncle Ali lol). I learned the offside rule myself after that, and used to read the local pink and green papers on a Saturday night, haha! Tommy Wright scored twice and Paul Wilkinson got the other as we beat Spurs 3-0. I honestly can't remember how we played, but I'm guessing okay from the score!

BORO 0 — 0 SHEFFIELD UNITED
RIVERSIDE STADIUM, AUGUST 7TH 2009
LEANNE LITTLEWOOD

My first experience of a live match wasn't until I was in my late 20s. I had always watched it on the TV but never actually been to the stadium. My dad had been a bit of a naughty boy at football matches when he was younger and always tried to keep us away from the environment that he remembered being part of, so we never ever went to the match as a family like I know many people do.

I do remember my first game though – it was the first appearance of Leroy Lita, August 7th 2009. He had joined Middlesbrough on a free transfer and we played against Sheffield United which finished up 0-0. I remember being really disappointed at the lack of goals especially since Leroy had the same initials as me which should surely mean that he was marvellous lol (I knew nothing at all about football at that point).

I spent the match sitting in the West Stand box area, having enjoyed a meal and drinks with some colleagues from Carlsberg who had provided me with two complimentary tickets.

My uncle came along with me and declared me bad luck, never to be allowed to come again. Unfortunately my bad luck streak continued – every match I attended over the years (it was only a handful), we lost.

I had never ever seen the Boro win until

my first away match which was Sheffield Wednesday in 2015. My bad luck effect on the Boro is well known within my family but I had somehow managed to be allowed to go along. The streak was finally broken and we battered Sheff Wed with three triumphant goals – Reach, Fabrini and Stuani. I finally experienced the thrill of a win and it was electric. Another memory of that match was a Sheff Wed fan who was a rather large fella taking off a lot of his clothes and screaming at the away fans. I can't remember the chant but I recall being very impressed by how loud he managed to be in the short time before he was physically ushered away from his soap box by the stewards and police.

BORO 3 – 1 PLYMOUTH ARGYLE
AYRESOME PARK, 1988
LEIGH FISHER

My first Boro match was v Plymouth Argyle back in 1988. It was for my tenth birthday pressie so would have been around April, after the FA Cup matches v Everton. We won. I remember it was 3-1. Big Alan Kernaghan, Gary Hamilton and Stuart Ripley scored. I remember excitement as we had been playing all of them FA Cup matches v Everton and finally getting to meet the players. I had Sports Gazette posters to get signed. Most of the players seemed to have bleached blond hair apart from Mark Burke, Paul Kerr and Bernie Slaven. My seat was in the East End Stand, the Boys Stand behind the goal. I never got the chance to go in the Holgate. I wish I did now but I was always in the East End seats until 1992, then I swapped to North Stand Upper before I moved to lower behind the Dial a Duck dugout which I climbed on the last game against Luton Town.

I always remember how I started getting into players' autographs when I got invited onto the Man Utd bus by Alex Ferguson and meeting Mark Hughes, Bryan Robson, Paul McGrath, Brian McClair, then it started being a regular when I moved to the North Terrace. Barry, the concierge gate man always let me stand in corridors, that's where I got chatting to Gordon Cox and Alastair, then Eric Paylor when the journalist room used to be opposite the home team changing rooms and players used to go in the players' clubroom which was downstairs too.

BORO 2 – 0 BURY
AYRESOME PARK, SATURDAY NOVEMBER 23RD 1963
LEIGH SAYERS

I was eight years old.

1. Eddie Connachan
2. Cyril Knowles
3. Gordon Jones
4. Ray Yeoman
5. Billy Gates
6. Billy Horner
7. Arthur Kaye
8. Ian Gibson
9. Brian Orritt
10. Bill Harris
11. Don Ratcliffe

Att 15,815

Gibson scored after 7 minutes and Orritt added the second on 28 minutes. We scored a third in the second half but it was disallowed for offside. It was never offside!

My uncle took me to this first game. I think he drove his little grey Morris from my grandma's house at Belle Vue and parked in Westminster Road. We sat in the North Stand, the only time I ever did that for a first team game. The same uncle took me to an Under 21 game against East Germany around this time but I was soon going to matches with my pals and standing in the Boys End.

BORO 2 – 2 SWINDON
AYRESOME PARK, DECEMBER 1991
LIAM LEMON MCARDLE

My first Boro game I attended was December 1991 v Swindon at Ayresome Park. I remember feeling excited but also nervous as I didn't know what to expect. The walk to the stadium was a strange one, just walking past people's houses then there it was. Once in the stadium, it was an unknown feeling, nothing I'd ever felt before, but as soon as the match kicked off everything felt right. As well as watching the game I would be listening to the fans singing. And in my head trying to remember all the words to the different songs. My favourite was, "We shall overcome." I think it showed me the fighting spirit that the fans had. They knew that one day we would succeed. And we did. I remember Wilko and Slaven getting the goals in a 2-2 draw. I can't really remember how well we played, but they must have done some good because I went back again.

BORO 0 – 2 LEICESTER
RIVERSIDE STADIUM, 1996
LIZ TAYLORSON

Ah, the 1970s. Every Saturday morning my mum would rush to check the fixture list in the Yorkshire Post to see if Boro were playing at home. If they were, we'd avoid going anywhere near the town centre that day, for fear of running into any visiting hooligans at the train station. That's why I didn't attend my first football match until I was well into my twenties, in 1996.

When I did, I wasn't even living in

Middlesbrough. I was in Durham, and I had made friends with a lifelong Boro fan who was appalled that despite coming from the Boro I had never been anywhere near Ayresome Park in my entire life. He said, "You'll enjoy it." Remembering my mum's terror of football hooligans, I said, "I don't think so!" He said, "I'll prove it ..." and so I ended up in the Upper West Stand of the Riverside, with a group of his friends, on a December night in 1996, with somewhat mixed expectations.

I expected to be cold, which I was, but I also expected to be bored, which I wasn't. I had expected football to be slow, dull and very muddy, and I had expected impenetrable rules (I mean, the offside rule is a standing joke, right?) that would render the match unwatchable to a novice like me. I found none of that was true. The sheer scale of the stadium took me by surprise. The colour, the bright lights, the roar of the crowd, even the smell (a mixture of cold grass, cigarette smoke and pies) all hit me at once and it was exciting. This was something big, something important, something that people cared about. Within about five minutes of kick-off, I suddenly and unexpectedly found that I cared about it too. It didn't matter that I didn't understand the details, the game itself was simple – the red team needs to get the ball in the net of the blue team, and the red team are our team. It doesn't get much more elemental than that, really, does it?

Can I confess something? When I sat down to write this piece, I was convinced that Boro had won my first football match. I remembered it vividly. I remembered the exhilarating feeling of a goal being scored, I remembered jumping to my feet and cheering as part of a celebrating crowd, I remembered feeling that this is my team, my goal, my victory, I had come home… only to discover when I checked the statistics that Boro had lost 2-0 to Leicester. Memories, as well as expectations, can be proved wrong!

BORO 0 – 1 ARSENAL
AYRESOME PARK, MAY 6TH 1989
LOUISE WILKIN

My first Boro match was against Arsenal on May 6th 1989, the last home game of the 1988/89 season. I wasn't originally going to go – my parents had a call that morning from friends who were going away, asking if they wanted to use their Season Tickets? I must have sulked loads as my mam said she felt poorly (I don't think she did really) and said I should go with my dad instead. I was so excited!

I remember the anticipation as we walked through the busy streets approaching Ayresome Park and then, as we came to the top of the stairs in the upper tier of the North Stand, the bright green pitch dazzling in the Saturday afternoon sunlight.

We lost 0-1 (Martin Hayes was their goalscorer), but to be honest, I don't remember much else about the game itself, other than the stick that Tony Adams took from the Holgate End (and the coconut mushrooms that my dad and I shared from a white paper bag in his pocket).

The season ended shortly afterwards in Boro's relegation after just one season back in the First Division (while Arsenal won the league title), but I was hooked!

BORO V WEST HAM
AYRESOME PARK
MACKENZIE THORPE

First Boro match at Ayresome Park was with West Ham and to see the great Bobby Moore play. It was the early 1970s, and I had never been before (always more into drawing and painting) but you can't be from Middlesbrough and not get caught up in the ups and downs of the Boro! I remember being really excited. More than the match itself, I remember the atmosphere, the laughter, the sounds of singing, the gasps at the near misses, the bright green of the pitch and walking there. There seemed to be thousands of people (seemed to be mainly men then) with red and white scarves all walking in the same direction and people would nod or acknowledge you as a fellow supporter. I felt like I belonged, the sense of community was nice and those memories are still strong. I suppose that is what influences me.

BORO 0 – 2 SHEFFIELD WEDNESDAY
AYRESOME PARK, NEW YEAR'S DAY 1991
MARK BENTON

I think it was Sheffield Wednesday. Basically I wasn't into football when I was a kid because my dad wasn't into football and no one in my family were, really. My brother had a Leeds pencil case but that was about it. I was friendly with Marcus Bentley, the Voice of Big Brother. He always threatened to take me to a match. And he took me to one on New Year's Day. I must have been sixteen or seventeen. He took me and we stood at Ayresome Park. We lost but I loved it.

I remember seeing these couple of gadgies and one of them was crying and that was it really, I never looked back. I almost cursed that I had never got into it before that and then I couldn't get enough of it. Some people say they don't like football but you ask them if have they ever been to a match and they say no. You say, don't say you don't like football 'til you've been to a match. It is different when you are there.

From then on, we got Season Tickets and I used to drive up from London just for the match most of the time. Yes, I loved it and I have ever since.

WEARING PJS SO I WOULDN'T GET COLD
AYRESOME PARK
MARK 'CLEM' CLEMMIT

I've got such a clear image of the events surrounding my first ever Boro match. It was the late 1960s. My dad making me wear pyjamas under my clothes, so I wasn't cold. Then afterwards, as guests of one of the directors at the time, looking out of a smoky boardroom window onto the crowds on Warwick Street.

In my head, the opposition that day were Burnley. I swear I can picture their claret and blue. Yet around that time they weren't in our division, nor West Ham and if it was games against Aston Villa in 1967 or 1969, they were both in late summer, so why the pjs?

BORO 3 – 1 WALSALL
AYRESOME PARK, SEPTEMBER 1986
MARK DRURY

My first Boro match was in 1986, in the September I think, as Boro beat Walsall 3-1 at Ayresome Park. I haven't checked the scorers but I think it was Archie Stephens, Stuart Ripley and Bernie Slaven. Mark Prudhoe was in goal for Walsall and I remember Archie Stephens leaving his boot somewhere in Prudhoe's back as he went up for a header in front of the Holgate End. Our dad took me through the Ayresome gates and we sat in the lower tier of the North Stand, to the right of the tunnel as we looked at the pitch (so nearer the Holgate than the East End), not far from the 18 yard line. I was eight years old and had been wanting to go to the match for what seemed like forever! I have a vivid recollection of the toilets in the corner, next to the steps up to the stand and that first sight of the Ayresome turf is one that will never leave me. I was smitten immediately. The crowd was probably in the region of 5-6,000 (it was early in the Division 3 promotion season) but that was the biggest number of people I'd ever seen in one place. A bright, sunny day and one of the happiest memories of my life, to this day. I'll never forget it.

BORO 3 – 3 SOUTHAMPTON
AYRESOME PARK, SATURDAY APRIL 8TH 1989
MARK MOTLEY

I have actually just realised my first Boro game was against Southampton and not Tranmere Rovers as first thought. This was on Saturday 8th April 1989 and the result was an action packed 3-3 draw.

At the time I was seven years old, a couple of months off being eight. I was actually taken to the game by my next door neighbour as my dad is not a football fan. Our neighbour Colin, no longer with us, was a massive fan, so he took me along.

I remember getting on the bus from

Ormesby Bank (just near the Pied Piper pub we lived close to). I remember walking from Middlesbrough Bus Station up Linthorpe Road and then weaving in and out of the streets around Ayresome to get to the ground and seeing all the people waiting to get in and buying burgers from the vans outside. We sat behind the goal in the East End seats, it was a good view, plenty of space. Attendance was around 16,000 that day.

From the day I vividly remember for quite some time just watching the Holgate and was fascinated by the amount of people singing and jumping up down. I also remember the awful toilet facilities.

In terms of the match, Boro scored on the 45th minute via Gary Hamilton and then Rod Wallace equalised on 75 minutes. Following that, Bernie scored and then Mark Burke both on 90 minutes, to give us a 3-1 lead. Neil Ruddock then scored two in injury time to get the draw.

After that game I think I was hooked with the drama and the Holgate.

BORO 0 – 2 FULHAM
AYRESOME PARK, SEPTEMBER 2ND 1973
MARK UNDERWOOD

My first match was the first home game of the 1973/74 season on September 2nd 1973. We lost 0-2 to Fulham. I remember that I was taken by my dad's best friend Ken, as my dad was working in the USA. We sat in a seat and I think that it may have been a slightly delayed eleventh birthday present. I recall a lot of hopeful expectation before the game and then Ken telling my Mum something like, "Useless and never again," after it.

As a young boy living in Middlesbrough, football was by far the most popular sport and being born and bred in Middlesbrough there was only one team that I could support. I was desperate to attend a live match and to see the players like John Hickton, Willie Maddren and Stuart Boam who we pretended to be in our playground games at school.

Whilst I would love to comment on the fervent atmosphere, and the individual players performances, truth be told I can't remember anything about the game as it was so long ago.

I do know though that I felt that going to 'the match' for the first time was an important rite of passage. Some of my friends, and one in particular, Robert Nichols, had already been to a match as his dad had a couple of Season Tickets and I suspect that I was jealous. I also know for a fact that, despite the result, I couldn't wait to go back, and I think my next match was standing in the Boys End with Robert Nichols when someone else was using his dad's second Season Ticket but his dad was able to give us a lift to and from the ground. I also remember having to tell my mum that I was going to sit in the stand with Robert and his dad when we were actually going in the Boys End as otherwise I would not have been allowed to go.

Writing this has made me compare and contrast my first visit to Ayresome Park, aged eleven, with the first visit to the Riverside of my daughter and son (who shared a Season Ticket at the Riverside from the ages of five and four respectively). How football has changed over the intervening years – for the better! I can't imagine being happy taking a four-year-old to Ayresome Park in the 1970s but it felt perfectly safe to start indoctrinating my children into Boro fans by taking them to the Riverside from an early age.

BORO 5 – 0 ARSENAL
AYRESOME PARK, MAY 19TH 1980
MARTIN JOHNSON

I was in Fort William, the wooden fort, at Lightwater Valley on the afternoon of Monday May 19th 1980. It started to rain which cut the day short, and when we go back into the car, dad suggested we might go to the match on the evening, my first game against Arsenal which was due to have been played back in February but for some reason it was postponed, no idea why. And so that night we went off to Ayresome Park. We parked on Gifford Street, which was where we used to park each week for years. I remember walking to the ground and seeing the bright floodlights, I still remember the feeling to this day. We stopped at the small sweet shop on the corner, which I think would have been on Clive Road. We wandered down and I vividly remember getting through the turnstile, maybe a 'squeezie,' and wanting to go straight up the steps in the South Stand because that was where the action was but my dad wanted to go to the toilet, so I stood waiting. I can still remember watching people streaming in and the sights and the smells. It seemed such a grown-up place, with smoking and swearing going on!

We went in and I saw the pitch. I remember saying something like, "It's greener than I thought it would be," or something along those lines. And it was a fantastic experience. I've still got the programme here. We won five nil and I've got the scorers because my dad wrote them on the back: Craig Johnston, David Hodgson, Graeme Hedley and David Armstrong, with two.

I seem to remember that Arsenal were below par having just won something. The crowd was 15,603 and there's loads of good references of the time in the match programme and ticket with the subs pencilled in on the back. One pound twenty including VAT (!) to get in.

It's a really good memory now forty years

ago despite proving to be an awful time for the club towards 1986. The South Terrace, the Chicken Run, home for my dad, my bespoke bracket seat that would fit onto the crash barrier and me sat way higher than any fresh faced nine-year-old should be!

Top Dad award to Colin for taking me for years and rationing the sweets for each half, a good life lesson until it was time for the Holgate End. I'm a Season Ticket to this day. It's in the blood, as the saying goes.

BORO 4 – 2 WOLVERHAMPTON WANDERERS
AYRESOME PARK, AUGUST 19TH 1989
MATT SMITH

You never forget your first love. It stays with you, through thick and thin, agony and elation and everything in between. You never forget your first time. The picture may be hazier and more blurred as the years pass you by. But the image remains. A constant feeling. A polaroid packed neatly away in the corner of your mind.

My first match was on August 19th 1989.

Wolverhampton Wanderers. The first game of the eventful end of Bruce Rioch's heroic reign. The slide. I'd arrived late to the party, but spirits were high as I took what would be my usual seat under the 'U' of the Bulkhaul sign in the North Stand lower. The Season Ticket had been my gift from my parents for my ninth birthday. I entered the ground alone and was met by my companions, some of my mum's friends.

Looking back, I'm taken by just how hard it must have been for my parents to agree to the Season Ticket and the seating arrangements at a time when Hillsborough was very much still taking up much of the back (and front) pages of the national tabloids and hooliganism was still very much a stain on the game. But, I can only assume, the months of constant pestering must have paid off.

It was like entering a new world. New sights. An oasis of pure, lush green set within a grey grid of oppressive terraced houses. New smells. Tobacco, Bovril, ammonia. New sounds. The Holgate End. A sea of swaying bodies and voices underpinning the atmosphere like an air raid siren. Grown men, gnarled and merry, singing together in unison. Chants, songs, cheers. Joy. Anguish. Anticipation. Calm.

It was a rousing victory, too. A 4-2 triumph. As we left our seats at the close, I remember looking up and asking my companion, "Is it like this every week?" She looked down at me with a kind of half-smile I now recognise, but didn't back then.

That's what it does to you. That's your first love.

BORO 1 – 1 WATFORD
RIVERSIDE STADIUM, MAY 6TH 2000
MATTHEW GALE

My first Boro match I seem to remember was against Watford at the Riverside (never went to Ayresome unfortunately) however I was only very young at the time so I couldn't remember exactly when it was although I distinctly remember Hamilton Ricard playing. I did a bit of research and the only fixture that fits that is May 6th 2000, when I would have been five.

I was born and raised in Leeds so didn't go

to many matches as a child, and also, in the strange thought processes children had, as a child I was scared of going to football matches as I thought the players were robots who were going to kill me! (No idea where that came from but it's been a running joke from my parents throughout my lifetime).

I remember pulling up to the McDonalds about half a mile from the stadium and having a Happy Meal in there (this is still to this day where my dad or I park the car for a match) and then walking to the stadium.

Turns out that match was a 1-1 draw with Robbie Stockdale scoring the goal for Boro, but as you can probably appreciate aged five at the time it was fairly blurry!

BORO 4 – 1 OXFORD
AYRESOME PARK, 1966/67
MAZ WIECZOREK

My memory is really poor about many things, then not bad about a few others!

I really can't remember for certain my very first game – but I DO have memories of the famous Boro v Oxford end of season promotion match, 4-1 victory, 1966/67.

It was a big 'treat' for me to go to the game with my dad – because it was a night time game too. I will have been about ten years old then.

I remember being almost 'carried' along with the massive crowd on the way in – but it scared the hell out of me, because I was so small. And I think my dad was also worried because he was trying to protect me.

The game itself was brilliant (I seem to think we scored more than 4 during the course of the game, but only 4 counted? Or did I dream that? I have this thing in my head of 8!)

I can clearly see Dickie Rooks rising high to head home from a corner? (But it was disallowed – or I've imagined it!)

I can remember the pure joy emanating from everyone at the end – dancing and hugging. But again, a little bit of terror trying to get out safely at the end – the lighting wasn't the best just outside the ground. I'm almost sure we were in the Bob End (East Stand), to the left of the goal, pretty high up?

The other very vivid memory from possibly that same season, or the next one – was someone pinching my brand new (hand-knitted) scarf from my neck, as they ran past me! And me and my dad couldn't do anything about it – he was too quick.

I was DEVASTATED!

BORO 1 – 0 WEST BROMICH ALBION
AYRESOME PARK
MEL SMALL

It was against West Brom in the seats at the old place and Boro won one nil. The original super sub Peter Barnes was playing for the Baggies. I must have been about eight or nine and our next door neighbour took my dad and I. The neighbour was called Ken James. My dad's name was Bill Small.

To my shame I was a Liverpool fan back then and Ken James, the neighbour, used to joke over the fence that they were just Boro rejects.

BORO 2 – 0 DERBY
AYRESOME PARK, 1977
MICHAEL READMAN

It was January or February 1977 so I was twelve and was round at a friend's house late Saturday morning when his dad asked if we fancied going to the match, Boro were playing Derby. I had to run home and check it was okay, have a quick lunch and back to my friend's. We sat in the East End (£1.20), a programme was 10p (which I think I still have) and we won 2-0. The historic moment in the match was David Armstrong missing a penalty for the first time in his career although someone was on hand to tuck the rebound in. I think it was in front of us but wouldn't put money on it. The thing that amazed me was how accurate the passing was, nothing like what I was used to at school!

Afterwards, was a visit to the club shop to buy a team poster for another 10p, what a day.

My dad had no interest in football, a bit like me now, so was mightily relieved when the minister of our church in Northallerton heard of my interest and asked if I would like to go up fairly regularly with him, his son (who will have been in his 20s) and an ex-neighbour of ours. That same season I think I saw us beat Tottenham 2-0, Arsenal 4-1 in the cup and draw 0-0 with Bristol City last game of the season. How great did I feel, sat in the car with three grown-ups all chain-smoking their way twenty miles up there.

The minister moved away at the end of the season so it was back down to dad. He took me and a friend to the Leeds home game (2-1), East End again near all the bother in the corner, and was just settling down to do his crossword when it all went dark due to everyone standing to celebrate an early Boro goal. Later that season he drove me and the minister's son up for another match and paid him in just so that he didn't have to take me. My only other one that year was Coventry 3-0 in the 3rd Round of the FA Cup and David Mills' Shoot goal of the season. I think that my only experience of dad 'enjoying' a game was November/December 1978 when we hosted Chelsea and gave Danny Blanchflower a polite reception before beating them 7-2 with Micky Burns getting 4.

BORO 2 – 2 NOTTINGHAM FOREST
AYRESOME PARK
MICK RICHARDSON

My first game was with my dad but I was too young. We played Forest and drew 2-2 so I'm told. I was happy enough until Boro scored and the noise from the crowd scared me so much I started crying. Dad edged toward the back of the stands so he could still watch but when Boro scored again I called time and we left early.

I started going on my own in 1986. Main Stand Season Ticket. Funny thing is, I never attended a match with my dad again. He just fell out of love with Boro. Poor bloke missed all the cup runs, Europe, Juninho…

LIVERPOOL 0 – 2 BORO
ANFIELD, 1976
MICK STEAD

First Boro game I actually attended was more or less a home game for me (living in North Wales) when we won 0-2 at Anfield in 1976. In fact, John Hickton's goal that day ranks among my favourite Boro goals even though there was nothing particularly special about it. I asked him about it outside the club shop recently and he said he couldn't even remember it! Cooper's 50 yarder in that game was far more spectacular even if Clemence did fumble it a bit.

First home game was later in the year (1976) when we beat Coventry at Ayresome Park with a Tony McAndrew goal. It might have been the first time he'd played at number 9, if I remember correctly. Anyway, I'd been at Acklam Park earlier that morning for the Yorkshire v Glamorgan County Championship game. Everyone was excited by the prospect of seeing Boycott bat, if you can believe that.

As it was, Glamorgan batted first and Alan Jones had scored 100 by the time I left for Ayresome Park along with many others. This was a bit of an odd coincidence because I'd actually been in Glamorgan CCC nets led by Alan Jones at various times. Suffice to say, it was a fantastic day of first class sport in Middlesbrough. Terrible shame Acklam Park lost the county fixture.

YORK CITY V BORO
BOOTHAM CRESCENT, LEAGUE CUP, 1971
MICK THOMPSON

My first attendance at a Boro match was an away game. It was the Second Round of the League Cup against York City at Bootham Crescent in 1971. It was the time when football hooliganism was dominating the news headlines. I remember us all being asked to leave the coach we were on, to allow the police to search the vehicle for alcohol.

My first game at Ayresome Park was on Saturday 8th January 1972 when we played Bristol City who had Dickie Rooks in their squad. I had gone along more out of curiosity than any other motive, and agreed to accompany my mate who lived next door, he was a Leeds 'fan'. This being the '70s I was in awe of the then Chelsea team featuring Charlie Cooke, Peter Osgood and Peter Bonetti. Middlesbrough Football Club didn't have the same appeal to the sixteen-year-old me, I'm now ashamed to admit. My delayed attachment to the mighty reds was partly the fault of my dad. He announced one Saturday morning that he had tickets for me and my brother to see Boro v Aston Villa. This would have been my first game, an important rite of passage in my dad's eyes. My love of football however had begun to wane as I discovered the hitherto mysterious attraction of female company. I had arranged to meet a lass in town and was determined that nothing would prevent me from my first date, not even the lure of an afternoon's football. My dad was horrified that I could even consider rejecting his offer in favour of a girl. I ran from the house, a decision I later regretted.

Back to the game in question. I can remember all around me hearing the moans and groans of men (they were mainly men) who longed for a return of the golden years of Mannion, Hardwick and Fenton and were clearly unimpressed with what filled the red shirts in those days. This was a view reinforced by my dad who had vowed never to attend a Boro game again following the transfer of his idol, Brian Clough. It seemed that the fans were resigned to their fate of mid table mediocrity.

We had seats in the front row of the main

stand and I remember being surprised at how close we were to the pitch, you could hear the players swearing at each other! My experience of football up until that point had been via television, and in black and white. I remember being fascinated with the vivid colours all around me adding to the spectacle of a live game. The bright green of the beautiful playing surface against the red shirts of my hometown team. I didn't miss a home game for the rest of that season, or for many of the following seasons, so the experience clearly affected me. I was smitten and my passion for my beloved Boro took root and has remained with me to this day. Who could have foreseen the emotional rollercoaster ride I was about to embark upon.

EATING A PIE AND WONDERING WHEN THE MEAT WOULD BEGIN...
AYRESOME PARK
MIKE BAKER

I like to say my first Boro match was the 6-0 drubbing of Leicester in 1990. Football seemed very easy that afternoon; my dad claimed it wasn't always this good, but what did he know? In reality though, I was taken years before as a bairn. The magic did not strike. I can't remember a thing about the game, indeed all I can recall is eating a match pie and wondering when the jelly finished and the meat began. People talk about their first experience of visiting a ground as something misty-eyed, mythical even – the smells, the manly camaraderie, the undercurrent of pent-up frustration and violence. I can't tell you anything about that. I was bored and I hated it.

BORO 1 – 1 CHELSEA
AYRESOME PARK, SEPTEMBER 1974
MIKE HENDERSON

We drew 1-1 (an early and rare Willie Maddren goal was cancelled out by an Ian Hutchinson equaliser). We sat directly behind the goal in the old East End. I was six. Much to my embarrassment, my father revels in telling the story that at one point I stood up and, apropos of nothing (and at a relatively quiet point)

shouted, "C'mon Boro, Chelsea are poofs!" (!!)
That story has probably aged as well as I have.
(I also remember asking my Dad if "****" was
swearing in the car home after a game when I
was young after hearing it in the ground! Cue
much squirming in the front of the car).

On a similar note, my son's first game was
in 2006 ,a week before his fourth birthday. He
hated it, was bored stiff and we lost 3-2 at home
to Wigan in a dreadful game with a 93rd minute
winner for the visitors. I think the highlight of
the game for those around me was me saying to
him very loudly after the final whistle "…and
son, if you're ever naughty again, I will bring
you back here for another game."

My daughter's first game was a couple of
years earlier. I had primed the guy who sat next
to me (I was row 20, seat 85 in the North Stand
so right in the middle) that I was bringing my
five-year-old to the next game and that if he
could swear less I'd appreciate it. He said he
had a young niece, fully understood, and would
be on his best behaviour. I brought Annie,
Boro shirt on, red and white bobbles in her
pigtails and sitting on a car booster seat to have

any chance of seeing. For five minutes the guy next to her (let's call him Simon, as that was his name!) was perfectly behaved. Cue a sliced clearance from Mark Schwarzer, followed by (at the top of his lungs) Simon yelling "**** hell Schwarzer, you Australian ****!" Annie has never been the same.

BORO 9 – 0 BRIGHTON HOVE ALBION
AYRESOME PARK, SATURDAY AUGUST 23RD 1958
MIKE MCCANN

The first Boro match at Ayresome Park I remember in any detail was the famous home game of the 1958/9 season played on Saturday 23rd August 1958 against Brighton Hove Albion, newly promoted Champions of Division 3. It was a glorious sunny afternoon, my mate Pete Morgan and I walked from the Whinney Banks via Acklam Garden City to West Lane then through Linthorpe Cemetery (passing the grave of Fred Hardisty, founder member, player and first chairman of MFC), making our way to the ground along with over 32,000 other fans.

Brian Clough played centre forward, alongside him Alan Peacock, with Billy Day on the right wing and Eddie Holliday on the left. Peter Taylor was in goal, Ray Bilcliff, Bill Harris and Brian Philips in defence. Billy Day, Army Sprint Champion, was flown home every weekend from Germany where he was stationed during his two years National Service. Eddie Holliday, a skilful left winger, gained his first England cap the following season along with Brian Clough (they played together in the goalless Wales v England International on October 17th 1958, I was there!). So the Boro front line up was brimming with talent that day.

During the summer Brian Clough had complained to manager Bob Dennison about the team's poor defensive record and suspected that some players were involved in match fixing. Dennison rejected the accusation but promoted Cloughie to captain at the start of the season.

The new captain scored five goals that day! I remember Billy Day sprinting down the right wing and putting in a cross about knee high; Clough swung his right leg and hit it first time straight into the back of the net! If I remember correctly, Billy repeated his run later in the game and Clough scored an identical goal from the pass! Up and coming Alan Peacock scored two goals and Bill Harris converted two penalties; final score 9-0. No defensive mistakes, what a fantastic start to the season!

As we walked home through the cemetery, there was much animated discussion with fans about our promotion prospects to Division One. However it was not to be. Boro went nine games before another win. At the end of the season, despite Brian Clough being the League's top scorer with 42 goals, Boro finished in thirteenth position, one place below Brighton.

Cloughie continued his protests about the dodgy defence which led to the team's 'Round Robin' signed by nine players asking for him to be relieved of the captaincy in November 1959. I was at the next home game against Bristol Rovers where Cloughie answered his critics – by scoring a hat trick!

(Wales v England 17th October 1958 – Mick McNeil got some tickets for us, one of my mates was a school

pal of his, so we made an overnight train journey to Cardiff to watch the match and came back home after the match with another overnight train journey!)

HEREFORD UNITED V BORO
EDGAR STREET, 2ND ROUND 2ND LEG LEAGUE CUP, FEBRUARY 6TH 2016
MIKKEL BECK, FORMER BORO PLAYER

I remember the game very, very well. I scored, I think with my right foot. I can't remember if it was actually Jan (Aage Fjortoft) that flicked it on but Jan became one of my very best friends that season and he really put his arm around me, he is a bit older than me. We are both from Scandinavia, so his family became a very important family for me and my integration. So, it was nice to finally play up front with him and him setting me up for my goal was brilliant. And it just went from there.

BORO 3 – 0 BANIK OSTRAVA
RIVERSIDE STADIUM, 2004
VLADIMIR JANAK AKA MIRO

In 2004 Banik Ostrava, as Czech football champions, played in the UEFA Cup, where they met Middlesbrough FC. Banik's website was offline which made it much more difficult for Boro supporters to get all important information.

That's why I registered on fmttm as Banik_ Fan and posted my offer to help anyone who would need some information. Hundreds of email messages began to immediately fill my inbox. I tried to answer every single one of them, but it was simply impossible. Therefore, I decided to build a website for Boro fans where I published articles with advice on how to get to Ostrava from Prague, where to find accommodate, how much is food, taxi, and so on.

Later it all became huge. I rented one whole hotel for Boro fans and hired my own staff, as the owners had no one speaking English. I also rented a few coaches and sent them with my own stewardesses to pick Boro fans up from the airport in Poland. I set up Boro Embassy Miro's Team – people trained to welcome Boro fans on railway and bus stations, to assist them with accommodation, to book a safe and cheap taxi (I had a deal with a trusted taxi company with a fixed price of £2.50 for every ride, no matter how long it is).

Boro fans were excited for what I had done for them. They appreciated it so much, so they invited me and my son Jan to watch the first leg. They paid for our flight tickets and all other expenses. Such an extraordinary story about friendship between opposite fans was attractive for the mass media obviously. After my arrival I had to give many interviews to BBC, ITV and Sky Sports who covered all my stay (yeah, it wasn't so far from proper stalking?), local radio stations and newspapers (especially Evening Gazette).

At half time of my very first Boro match, I was invited onto the pitch where I was given a Boro shirt from the hands of Chris Tomlinson, British Olympic long jumper. Boro won that match 3-0. Ironically, I was watching my first Boro match as a supporter of the opposite side which lost the game. But I personally gained much more. I've got new fantastic friends, incredible memories and… yes, I've got a new home as I moved with my family to Middlesbrough more than two years ago. And my daughter just signed for Middlesbrough Women FC? Could that story end any better? UTB!

BORO 5 – 7 ENGLAND XI
AYRESOME PARK, HAROLD SHEPHERDSON TESTIMONIAL, MAY 7TH 1973
NEIL ALDRIDGE

I had the privilege of growing up in Marton just three doors away from Harold Shepherdson, so when his Testimonial was announced we just had to go. I could never support any other team, it had to be the Boro. Harold's testimonial was my first match, I was ten years old, it was a big day out with dad, and a full house. I knew it wasn't a real game, but I was seeing the players I'd heard so much about, and I saw goals. Twelve goals, not the usual Boro score. It was obvious even to me that some of the older players scored because defenders didn't defend, or the goalie let them in (although Dibble gave a similar performance at QPR in 98). I had the taste for real matches and we went to a few mid-week games; but every one was a predictable 0-0, and so for a few years it was only testimonials and the first is always the best. The first Riverside match was fantastic, and the first Wembley Cup finals were... (best to cut the theme at this point).

BEER FUMES AND CIGARETTES – MY FIRST ENCOUNTER WITH THE HOLGATE
BORO 2 – 1 WEST BROMWICH ALBION
AYRESOME PARK, OCTOBER 6TH 1979
NEIL GARRATT

My first match at Ayresome Park was October 6th 1979 v West Bromwich Albion. I was 10 stone soaking wet, I remember it well through a haze of beer fumes and clouds of cigarette smoke.

At home the day began with the ritual laying out of the Boro shirt, making sure the Levis were neat and the Adidas trainers clean and smart. The scarf was always left till last – it was one of those tacky acrylic things, with rubberised letters and the club crest with the ship.

Off to the pub for a wet and a warm: The Empire, Yellow Rose and The Westminster, in that order. Then, take up the spot in the middle of the Holgate: second crash barrier, just to the right of the left hand goal post. It had to be there, because if you were at the end of the barrier and we scored – you found yourself 'surfed' to the other side of the tin shed. Many a time you would end up far away from the position you started. One minute you're talking to your buddy and next you're amongst a group of elated but anonymous strangers. All held together by red and white.

Back to the game: John Neal was in the process of adding his own stamp to the Boro side, with a mixture of older pros and young players: big John Craggs and wily fox Mickey Burns, complimented Mark Proctor, Ian Bailey, David Hodgson and Craig Johnston in the starting line up. Ever-present 'Spike'

Armstrong and Tony McAndrew were on the field, with Jim Platt in goal, our 'Foreign International' 'Bosco' Jankovic, and finally, Billy Ashcroft - the ginger 'cruncher'. On the bench was a skinny Irishman who never pulled his socks up – Terry Cochrane.

The West Brom team that day included a midfielder who later became Boro Manager and brought the 'samba years' to the Riverside – Bryan Robson. Up front was David Mills, who Ron Atkinson had shelled out over £500,000 to the Boro before the season started.

Other notables were the much-travelled Peter Barnes, who always delighted with his pace down the wings, and Tony Godden in goal enjoying one of his three spells with the Baggies.

I remember it being one of those huff and puff matches, where one mistake or lapse of concentration would see the ball over the line. I wasn't wrong: the Wily Fox, Micky Burns, turned the ball into the net on half time to make it 1-0 to the Boro. At the time my teenage enthusiasm believed Boro could defend the lead for the next 45 minutes and the points were 'in the bag!' (Don't talk daft, I hear you say).

Big Bosco was replaced by Terry Cochrane at half time. We had chewed our nails down to the bone in a tense second half when Gary Owen equalised on 90 minutes! Before the ref blew for full time Spike scored at the other end to make it 2-1 Boro!!

Cue the mandatory surge down towards the touchline and "You are my Boro! My only Boro…" Ecstasy! The adrenaline flowed through my veins, along with the John Smith's Magnet and I was hooked! There was no way out! No return! The 16,000+ crowd sounded more like 30,000. The noise in the Holgate was deafening. Right up until our move to the Riverside I always stood in the Holgate: its unique atmosphere – beer fumes and cigarettes – the highs and lows. Singing, crying, feeling deflated one minute, then on top of the world the next. Welcome to the rollercoaster, son! UTMB.

BORO V LEICESTER
AYRESOME PARK, 1988
NEIL GRAINGER

My dad took me to my first Boro match against Leicester at the end of the 1987/88 season. Apparently, it was a must win game but I was totally oblivious and just thought all games were that tense. I vividly remember that walk to Ayresome Park and the feeling of nervous butterflies as the stadium came in to view. We watched the game down by one of the corner flags and against the big red cage. I spend the first half marvelling at the noise, the speed of Stuart Ripley and the size of Stephen Pears and his tash. It turned out that my first game ended up being my shortest game as my dad made us leave after 60 minutes. I remember being gutted to be made to leave so early and to this day, no matter how badly we are being beaten, I find it hard to leave before the whistle. It was my first of many trips to Ayresome Park and whilst I miss that atmosphere, I certainly don't miss that cage.

BORO 3 – 1 BLACKBURN ROVERS
AYRESOME PARK, FA CUP, MARCH 11TH 1963
NEIL WHELDON

I remember getting the N Bus from the top of Overdale Road, my buddy Fejie Myers gets the bus at Crossfell Road, the bus is ram jam full of Boro fans. Walking up Linthorpe Road, down Ayresome Street, millions of people swarming like flies to Ayresome Park. It was a Monday night, floodlights on. Queue up for Boys End in corner of Bob End. I thought it was called the Bob End because of all the people in it were called Bob but that's how much it used to cost to get in years before, equal to 5p today. Run up the concrete steps to the enclosure with notices on walls: WARNING BOYS MUST NOT CLIMB OUT OF ENCOSURE. The crowd of 39,595 (Thank you to Who's That Team They Call The Boro book) was one of the biggest crowds I would ever be part of at Boro. Loads of kids were climbing over the wall but the old gadgie end, as we called it, was so packed we decided to stay where we were. Alan Peacock scored 2 and Arfor Kaye scored and we won 3-1.

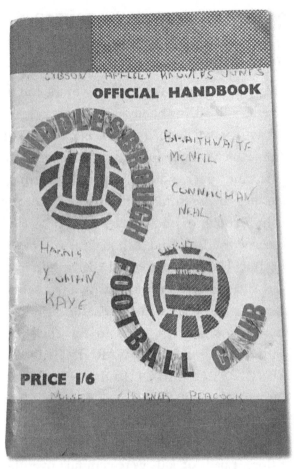

A kid from school called Fatty Young jumped over the wall and the lone steward grabbed him and said, "What's your name?" He replied, "Fatty Young," and ran off into the crowd. He called himself this because he was a trifle stout and was proud of the fact that he was the heaviest kid in class and was anchor man in the Langbaurgh v Springfield annual tug of war competition.

We had wooden rattles, they would be banned now, and we were singing, "We're on our way to Wembley," and "We shall not be moved." Little did we know that we would be grandads before we got to an FA Cup final and then our joy would only last for 44 seconds.

When I look back, so many important events in the world had not happened then. Curly Wurlys were not invented until 1970. Cliff Richard was number one in the charts with Summer Holiday, The Beatles did not hit top for another six weeks. Walking down Linthorpe Road in the dark was great. "Wembley, Wembley," was the chant, yet it was only Round 3. We would not have believed that 34 years later we would go to three Wembley finals in a row and lose them all.

Sitting on the bus I said to Fejie (his real name was Jeff but Fejie was Jeff in reverse, sort of), "I hope we get to Wembley before

IAN GIBSON
(I.F.) Ht. 5' 7". Wt. 10 st. 7 lbs. Born NEWTON STEWART. Although only 20 years of age, has played in League football for 5 years. As an amateur with Accrington and pro. with Bradford (P.A.). Signed from them in March 1962, for a large fee. Tipped to gain representative honours in near future.

ALAN PEACOCK
(C.F.) Ht. 6' 0½". Wt. 11 st. 7 lbs. Born MIDDLESBROUGH. Signed professional in 1954. For three seasons played at inside forward, but when switched to centre forward was so successful he was chosen for World Cup team 1962; capped against Bulgaria, Argentina. Last term 'capped' v. Ireland and Wales.

WILLIAM HORNER
(W.H.) Ht. 5' 7". Wt. 10 st. 12 lbs. Born CASSOP. Signed on Ground Staff in 1957 and became professional in September 1959. Has made quite a number of appearances for the First Team. A good solid defender who possesses a brilliant shot.

ARTHUR LIGHTENING
(Goalkeeper) Born Durban, South Africa. Ht. 6' 1". Wt. 12 st. 7 lbs. Previously with Notts. Forest—signed from Coventry City on 30th August, 1962. Injured in his first match against Newcastle, but later hit top form.

17

we are eighteen because then we will be too elderly to enjoy it." Fatty Young was on the bus and he said he could not see any goals in the old gadgie's end as it was packed out and someone dropped a bingie on his head (a bingie was a burnt-out end of cigarette that that was unceremoniously cast asunder by the smoker after he had finished with it, with no attention paid to the unfortunate Fatty Young) and a lot of people were Billy Wright-ing (breaking wind).

The joy and sorrow of watching Boro goes on and I still go now with Nigel and three grandsons. Got Alan Peacock's autograph that night and 54 years later Alan signed for grandson Jude and the signatures were exactly the same, good lad Alan.

BORO V WOLVES
AYRESOME PARK, THE HOLGATE END, 1978
NICK RAISTRICK

In an effort to separate me and my brother from the Highlander-style ongoing conflict in which we were locked until adulthood, he went to see Big Daddy wrestling at the Town Hall with my grandad. I got the football. We'd drive to nan's house in Linthorpe, where my granddad had put out cardboard boxes to ensure a parking spot, free parking being an important guiding principle to our dad. In later years he'd drive for what seemed like several years in the hunt for Middlesbrough's dwindling toll-free parking spaces. The Walk: everyone walking, streets which retrospectively seem like something between a Lowry painting and a Zombie movie, everybody out and heading in the same direction, the atmosphere electric, with a twist of genuine danger. Police horses were taller in them day. And often there was a fight too, or more often, a beating up, a circle of Adidas Samba whacking into someone's head is vivid. Don't tell your mam about that, son. Turnstiles. So many people. The first sight of the pitch, the greenest green you will ever experience. The unity of movement. The surge of the crowd and being genuinely frightened and excited by the goal; and genuinely frightened by the gothic horror of toilets, compared to which the wet markets of Wuhan are a modern and healthy space. Fortunately time spent here was limited as the surge seemed to carry you out if you dawdled.

Was I passed over the heads of adults? Or is that false memory syndrome? But the crush being part of a swaying shoal of people was real. Everything would change after this first game; and I can remember every detail, except who was playing. I think it was 1978, and I think it was Wolves. I was five.

BORO V WATFORD
AYRESOME PARK, OCTOBER 1970
NICK SMALL

I have the haziest of memories of my first Boro game. That is, my memories of the game itself. It was October 1970. I had just turned eight years old and we'd moved from Whinney Banks to just off Roman Road. I recall walking to the game with my dad, with crowds getting thicker as we neared Ayresome Park. Beer, cigarette smoke and the whiff of Bovril soaked the heavy atmosphere. I remember the excitement building before we even got to the turnstiles. We sat somewhere quite low down below the Longines clock.

I have no real recollection of the game other

than Watford played in yellowish colours. They had a player called Jenkins, who I think may have scored. My memory may be faulty... but I think he was what I later learned to describe as a lanky streak of p*ss. Downing and Laidlaw made a firm impression upon me... mainly for their 70s styling... but it seems they also scored. I also learned, from my dad, that Charlie Amer was a total tw*t (he used to park his roller up a few doors down from us, visiting family, I believe). Harold Shepherdson looked like my grandad.

The match was drawn, but that was it. I was a Boro fan from then on.

I STILL DO NOT KNOW HOW MY DAD PERSUADED MY MUM TO LET ME GO
AYRESOME PARK, 1966/67
NICK WAITES

From discussions with my late parents, I believe that my first visit to Ayresome Park was at some time during the 1966/67 season when I would have been five years old but unfortunately whilst I do know that I went to a few games I will never find out which ones other than I can still remember the memorable last game of the season when we beat Oxford United to seal promotion in front of god knows how many supporters.

My dad had had a Season Ticket in the North Stand wing (on the Holgate side) for a number of years and until I left Teesside to go to university in Bristol I watched all of my football at the ground with him, initially as a squeeze and sitting on his knee until I got my own seat.

We always travelled to the game with a guy who lived four doors from us and sat behind us for a lot of years. He was 'Dennis,' a friend of my dad's, who would cycle to the games and leave his bike at the home of a guy he got to know over the years who lived in Dorset Close (I think it was) which is where we always used to park on the guy's drive.

A lot of people recall climbing the Ayresome Park steps before seeing for the first time the hallowed turf but I have got to be honest when I say I cannot recall any of that and my only real recollections of the game (and I still do not know how my dad persuaded my mum to let me go to a night game at that age) was that as the game was coming to an end, more and more fans were spilling onto the track around the pitch especially in front of the South Stand until the wall in front of the stand collapsed due to the sheer numbers of fans.

I remember the last few minutes of the game, and even though it is more than fifty years ago, thinking that I hoped that my dad would let me come again the following season.

Needless to say he did and from that day on it was in my blood.

BORO 3 – 2 LEYTON ORIENT
AYRESOME PARK, 1973
NIGEL DOWNING

My first Boro game came at the end of the 1972/73 season against Leyton Orient. My dad had got tickets for the North Stand from a neighbour. I remember walking down Warwick Street towards the main gates, squeezing between red and white scarved strangers, unusually loud and boisterous for adults. Excitement and anticipation nearly overwhelmed me when from behind grey coats and corduroyed legs I glimpsed the lime green of the pitch. In our seats, programme carefully scanned, I tried to take it all in. The stands and crowds, so familiar from watching football on telly were suddenly real and amplified by the smells of beer and cigarette smoke, and the disconcerting noise of the supporters (and this was the North Stand).

The match itself was a blur, but I see in my mind's eye, a red shirted figure racing into the open space below me, defenders lost in his wake as he arrows towards goal. The crowd calls drop away and I imagine I can hear his studs in the turf, the beat of his heart, as the keeper rushes to meet him, then with a swing of his foot he cracks the ball goalwards, the net billows and the Holgate erupts. Amidst the din the name of the scorer is announced on the tannoy... "a hat trick for John Hickton!"

A number of years later I checked through Rothmans to see if all this was true. It turned out that it was. Boro won 3-2, Big John scored a hat trick and Derrick Downing got the goals for the visitors.

Now, anyone who knows anything about the Boro would be aware that the following season proved to be one of the most momentous in Boro's history. You would think that after that introduction my dad and me would make our way regularly to Ayresome Park to see Jack Charlton's Aces, but of course things seldom work out as you might expect. I decided to become a Leeds fanatic and dad preferred a Saturday pint in the Endeavour. It wasn't until the days of Bruce Rioch and Tony Mowbray that we atoned for the terrible error of our ways, standing side by side in the Holgate.

Oh and it gets better. Who was the neighbour my dad got free tickets from? It was Boro skipper, Stuart Boam!

BORO 3 – 1 ASTON VILLA
RIVERSIDE STADIUM, 2006/07
OWEN SWIFT

My first game was v Aston Villa in the 2006/07 season, I believe? I can't remember anything much about it, other than being small and in a wheelchair and every time the ball went near either goal everyone in front would stand up and block my view. I went with my mam and we still go to every game home and away now!

I remember more of my second game. It was Fulham, last game of the season and we won 3-1. I believe? I sat on the very first seat in the south west where the south is separated and becomes the West Stand. I could see everything, it was great. I had the police horses under me in the exit tunnel. The following season I bought my first ever Season Ticket after collecting pocket money off my grandad each week till I could afford one (£95) at the time and I think we played Blackburn in the first game of the season and I was MFC's special guest.

BORO V MANCHESTER UNITED
AYRESOME PARK, CLAYTON BLACKMORE'S
TESTIMONIAL, AUGUST 16TH 1994
PADDY DILLON

I was quite lucky to get on the Boro bandwagon at the start of the Robson Revolution. When I got to Ayresome, I remember being excited to see South Cleveland Garages written on the roof. I thought it was weird that so many in the Boro end clapped Man United's goals. And I remember looking out for Bryan Robson arriving late after kick off from his transfer tribunal duties that day, but only seeing someone else in a long dark coat who I think was just a club doctor. I wish I could say I fell in love with the bright green grass or that I quickly tipped future stars in Scholes and Beckham, but no, all I remember is the club doctor, weird clapping, and South Cleveland Garages.

BORO 1 – 5 PORTSMOUTH
AYRESOME PARK, SATURDAY SEPTEMBER 3RD 1949
PAM SLATER

I was twelve years old and I was taken to the match by my dad and big brother Tony where we met up with my grandad who was a lifetime Boro supporter. I was pretty much his favourite grandchild and he was overjoyed to see me at the match. Boro is for us a family obsession but sadly I am the last of the line. We sat in the South Stand Upper – our usual place but on days when there was a big crowd we went on to the South Stand terrace – I remember a home game versus Arsenal when I thought I was going to be totally crushed!

Boro lost 1-5 to Portsmouth but it didn't put me off. Our goal was scored by Peter McKennan (a penalty). Interestingly Lindy Delapenha was playing for the opposition and he joined Boro shortly afterwards and became a Boro legend. The team that day was: Rolando Ugolini, Dicky Robinson, Hepple (not further identified in place of George Hardwick), Harry Bell, Stan Rickaby, Ron Dicks, Johnny Spuhler, Peter McKennan, Alex McCrae and Geoff

Walker and of course my all-time favourite, Wilf Mannion – the Golden Boy.

Many years later I acquired a photocopy of the programme via someone who was selling the original on line – I was not at all savvy about buying things online and my offer was much too low. The seller took pity on me and sent me a photocopy as it had been my first Boro game!

My love for the Boro was born that day and remains with me. They are my team.

BORO 0-0 WIGAN ATHLETIC
AYRESOME PARK, MAY 6TH 1987
PAUL ADDISON

My first Middlesbrough game was at the end of the season that the club rose from the ashes and narrowly avoided going out of business – a grim time.

The story is an often told one – playing the opening game against Port Vale at Hartlepool United's Victoria Ground because the gates to Ayresome Park were padlocked – you know the drill.

Up until the end of that season I'd been a fan without going to a match – my dad and brother went on Saturday afternoons and I'd stay at home with my mam keeping a check on the scores thanks to Final Score on BBC One but I have to admit I was more interested in my Star Wars figures than anything that was going on on a football pitch. That all changed when dad suggested I go along for one of the most famous of goalless draws in the Boro's history.

As I recall it was a cool, damp night as we made our way from Thornaby to park the car up in the streets surrounding Ayresome Park. We went to one of the paper shops on St Barnabas Road for what became a traditional purchase of sweets – I always went for lemon bon bons. I remember being highly amused by the fact one of the streets leading to the ground was called Addison Road – it was meant to be!

We were in the South Stand Upper to watch the game – it went by in a blur. If I'm honest, I can't remember anything about it other than the wild celebrations at the end when the players came back out into the North Stand to applaud their adoring public. I can only imagine what it meant to Boro diehards that night – their club had almost died and I'm sure there were tears shed by grown men as a group of players who were barely more than boys, along with manager Bruce Rioch, etched their places in club folklore. I do remember feeling a bid giddy on the way back to the car and I was smitten.

A few of the squad that night have become close friends thanks to my job as a journalist covering the team for BBC Radio Tees – I went on to work alongside Gary Gill, Paul Kerr and Bernie Slaven in the commentary box and have interviewed most of the rest of the line-up in their roles as managers at various clubs down the years but one thing unites them all – they're Boro Icons.

BORO 5 – 0 NORWICH
AYRESOME PARK, FEBRUARY 6TH 1971
PAUL ARMSTRONG

I haven't bought a football programme for decades, but I have one from the first game I went to with my dad, aged just five. February

6th 1971: the editorial 'Ayresome Airs' contained quaint phrases like "we must make reference to Frank Spraggon's injury," "it will be a mystery forever how we did not come away from Millwall as handsome winners," and "we must redouble our efforts to attain our goal." Only Boris Johnson still talks like that, and he's usually lying.

Amongst those companies advertising in this gloriously flimsy and dated publication were Newboulds Pies, Jack Hatfield's famous Sports Shop with its 'largest stocks in the North', the greyhound racing at Cleveland Park, building firm CW Athey of Linthorpe Road (CW Athey junior was later to play cricket for Yorkshire and England) and poignantly, the shipbuilders Swan Hunter who were advertising a host of new jobs as part of an 'Expansion on Teesside'. A certain Elvis Costello song springs to mind.

My abiding memory is the colour of the spectacle. Boro were pre-hoop so it was all red, versus yellow, and a green to match the grass. We sat at the Boys End, which became our regular perch for a few years. I distinctly remember Kevin Keelan, Norwich's keeper, in the goal in front of us, with sculpted dark hair like the Milk Tray man off the telly, lots of smoking and everyone jumping out of their seats. The game finished Middlesbrough 5 (Downing (Derrick, not Stewart), Hickton (2), McIlmoyle, Laidlaw) Norwich 0, the first of a ridiculous run of about thirty home games I didn't see us lose, until QPR came and beat us in the top flight a few years later. Talk about getting a false impression of what lay in store.

BORO 0 – 2 LEICESTER
RIVERSIDE STADIUM, DECEMBER 1996
PAUL COATES

My first Boro game I think was December 1996, home against Leicester. We didn't have a Season Ticket, but our neighbours did, and they used to offer it to us now and again when they didn't go. I guess they didn't fancy watching a Boro team lacking Juninho and Emerson, against Emile Heskey and co. So I went with my dad. I was ten at the time. I remember us parking up on a grass verge somewhere I'd never been before, then walking through what seemed like wasteland for ages. I don't remember much about the actual game at all (had to google the lineups). But I remember the stadium just feeling like the biggest thing I'd ever been in. I imagine as a kid I'd never seen that many people in one place, the noise was so intimidating, but when I realised that was fellow Boro fans, I remember that first buzz of excitement. The stadium seems small these days in comparison to that memory. I also remember it being freezing (no change there then) and I remember my dad covering my ears when there was swearing going on. Since we lost 0-2 there was a lot of that, haha!

BORO V HUDDERSFIELD
AYRESOME PARK
PAUL 'FROSTY' FROST

I remember it clearly even though I was only eight or nine. It was an evening fixture at Ayresome Park against Huddersfield. We travelled from Stockton on the O bus and walked for what seemed to be miles to the stadium; I can still picture squeezing through the clunking turnstiles for the first time; the brilliant green pitch under the floodlights (I swear I could feel the heat from them); the smell of beer on the supporters' breath and counting the fag ends flicked onto the ash track surrounding the pitch.

Players included Don Radcliffe, Ray Yeoman, Bryan Orritt and a big lad I think was called Irvine. We won by a thumping margin and I went home happy. I'd become a Boro supporter which meant I was now a 'big boy'... even though the beer on my breath would have to wait a few years!

BORO 1 – 2 WATFORD
AYRESOME PARK, 1990
PAUL SMITH (MAXIMO PARK)

My first game was Watford, under the floodlights at Ayresome Park, in 1990. I won the tickets by ringing in to TFM with a correct answer (probably Bernie Slaven). My dad and I ended up in the Dickens Suite with some other competition winners – I think I borrowed my cousin's suit! There was a sweepstake on who would score the first goal, and we thought we had a bad deal when we got defender Simon Coleman. Obviously, he then went on to score and we won the sweep, but lost the match 1-2. We were meant to meet the players afterwards but they were upset after the loss, we were told. Luckily, we saw the injured Colin Cooper in the corridor outside our suite, and he was extremely nice and posed for a photo. I think Boro losing managed to set me up to not expect too much from going to the football! I still get a buzz from the floodlit pitch, though.

BORO 2 – 0 WREXHAM
AYRESOME PARK, LEAGUE CUP, SEPTEMBER 5TH 1972
PAUL THOMPSON

My first game was a 2-0 win over Wrexham in the League Cup on September 5th 1972. David Mills scored both goals in front of 5,808 people. I don't remember a thing about it. I only know because I had an old school book where I'd written about it. I don't know how many games I got to after that, but I was a regular for Jack Charlton's record breaking

1973/74 season. My dad used to take me to a smoke filled café on Linthorpe Road, filled with old men speculating whether Foggon would score. Boro had been promoted back to Division Two in 1967 but by 1974 hadn't been in the top flight since 1954, and their last promotion to Division One was in 1929, forty five years earlier. No wonder people were excited. After nearly fifty years my memories are vague and impressionistic. Walking up the steps to the Bob End and seeing the vivid green of the pitch. I remember being at the corner of the Bob End and North Stand when David Armstrong came to take a corner. I was amazed that the God-like Boro winger looked just like a normal man. The smell of the ink on the programmes brings it all back.

With 25,286 other people, I saw Boro beat Sheffield Wednesday 8-0 on April 20th 1974. Being young in the 70s means I also had a ringside seat for Rioch's double promotion, the Robson era, Cup Finals, promotions, relegations, the unforgettable highs of Cardiff, Rome, Basle, Steaua Bucharest, Eindhoven, and Karanka's promotion. Hopefully there's time to add a few more to my personal selection of Boro's greatest hits.

Work commitments mean I get to less than ten games a season as a fan. Obviously the rush of excitement isn't the same as it was, when I was eight years old climbing the steps of the Bob End for the first time. But the spark is still there, even the dog days of Tony Pulis failed to completely extinguish it. 66% of my children are now Boro fans, as Meatloaf rightly said, 2 out of 3 ain't bad. My youngest got the bug when we saw Boro lose 4-3 to the mighty Accrington Stanley in a pre season game a couple of years ago. The story continues.

BORO V IPSWICH TOWN
AYRESOME PARK, 1964
PAUL YOLE

My first Boro game was a pre-season friendly just before my twelfth birthday in 1964 against Ipswich Town, who had recently won the Division 1 championship. We had been living abroad and in East Yorkshire so I hadn't been able to go to any games previously.

My dad took me and we sat in the East Stand at Ayresome Park. I can still remember the smell of pipe tobacco.

Boro lost. It was the start of a slide that would see us relegated to the old Third Division at the end of 1965/66. Boro players to feature that day included Alan Peacock, Bryan Orritt, Bill Harris and Mel Nurse. I think Bob Appleyard was in goal and Mick McNeil at full back. The stringiest memory, apart from the tobacco smell, was the aerial leap and awesome power of 'Peach' heading the ball towards goal from beyond the penalty spot.

I was hooked and became one of the founding members of the Ayresome Angels in 1966/67. Number 127, from memory.

BORO V BRADFORD
AYRESOME PARK, SEPTEMBER 4TH 1984
PAULA BRACK

My first game was a Tuesday night game against Bradford, September 4th 1984. I went with my best friend from school, Adelle and her dad, John (my dad wouldn't take me, despite begging him to for many years). I remember going to the newsagent and getting a bag of Sports Mixtures (the originals!). Whilst it was early September, I remember it being cold but that might just be a memory of being told to wrap up with being out at night – that was the highlight – staying out late and getting home past my bed time! I specifically remember Gary Hamilton playing, as I fancied him, tash and all.

BORO 3 – 1 AJAX
AYRESOME PARK, FRIDAY AUGUST 11TH 1978
PETER BRACK

I was six years of age and I was walking past my infant school, Archibald School, heading towards Ayresome Park. It was 6.30pm and it was a lovely summer night. My two older brothers were in Portsmouth at that time with the Boys Brigade, I was too young to go, so as a treat my dad decided to take me on a short trip from Corder Road in West Lane to Ayresome Green Lane and then Ayresome Park. I don't think for a moment, at that time, that he realised how much that treat would affect the rest of my life.

The opponents that night for Middlesbrough Football Club were an exotically named team called Ajax of Amsterdam. That name didn't mean much to me then but I was just learning and developing my football knowledge that year. I remember watching my first FA Cup Final in May that year on the TV, Ipswich v Arsenal in which Roger Osborne scored the only goal of the game and had to be substituted for exhaustion. In the summer was the World Cup in Argentina 1978, the noise, the colour, the ticker tape and the 'bring, diddy, bring, diddy, bring, diddy, bring' of the BBC World Cup theme had me hooked.

Now, as I was walking past the cemetery and General Hospital towards the ground, this was real life, this was happening, this was my first football game. The crowd starting to get larger and there was a little less space. The shout if anyone needed a programme was a little scary and unexpected which made me jump a little inside every time they shouted it.

We got the programme, all 15p worth,

which I clutched to my tiny body like I had seen Charlie do in the film with his golden ticket, nobody was going to take this away from me. We went down the alleyway towards the Holgate End behind the hospital. The alley smelt awful and was shrouded in darkness, the sunshine blocked out as we went under what seemed like a small tunnel but I now realise was probably part of the club's offices. I squeezed my dad's hand a bit tighter. I was small and unsure what the hell was going on but my god I was excited and I still get that same exciting feeling as I walk towards and through a turnstile to this day.

We went through the turnstile., I would be using poetic license to say that I got a squeeze but I am writing this so I will say that I did. We didn't go up the steps towards the top of the stand as my dad was aware that was where all the 'Big Daft Lads' stood and one day I would earn my stripes to stand there but not today. He walked me round the corner which was next to the North Stand and the whole stadium came into view.

I am not sure of the attendance and trust

I have tried to check but it felt on the day to a child at least 100,000 people were in that stadium. The colours, the noise, the smells are something that never leave you. The excitement of being out past my bedtime, watching players on the pitch that I had just seen on my TV only weeks before was mind blowing.

I think and I am willing to be proved incorrect, Middlesbrough won 3-1 with Big Billy Ashcroft scoring twice, I believe once with his head full of his beautiful ginger perm.

I walked back home both elated and shattered, having been injected with a drug called football which I have been addicted to ever since. I went to the ground excited by the names of Piet Schrijvers, Frank Arnesen, Soren Lerby and Rudi Krol. But left falling in love with a team with the names of Jim Platt, Willie Maddren, David Armstrong, Billy Ashcroft and Terry Cochrane.

My life was never to be the same again.

BORO 1 – 0 MILLWALL
AYRESOME PARK, OCTOBER 7TH 1972
PETER BRINE, FORMER BORO PLAYER

I made my debut as sub against Millwall on October 7th 1972. We won 1-0 through a goal by Willie Maddren. Before the Millwall game I had been included in the squad a couple of times but not selected in the 12. The 1972/73 season was good for me considering the awful 71/72 season.

I had a cartilage operation in October 1971 and I never played again that season. So I was really raring to play in 72/73. I was playing up front for the reserves and I must admit I was playing well and scoring a few goals. Stan Anderson sat me down and he said he was considering trying me in the first team a couple of weeks before I made debut against Millwall. It's quite ironic really because Millwall were the team I disliked the most. I was born in Charlton, South East London and of course my team was Charlton Athletic and Millwall were our nearest rivals. So it was great to play against them and to beat them.

I came on at half time for Gordon Jones and

played wide right midfield. The game is a bit of a blur now but I really enjoyed it. Of course I was nervous but my team mates and the crowd gave me great support. It is a great feeling running on to the field with the crowd behind you. With it being my first game obviously the crowd hadn't seen me play so it's on your mind to try and not disappoint them and your team mates and of course the boss.

My parents were very proud, especially my dad who was from the Boro. Unfortunately they couldn't get up for the game but fortunately I was named as sub against Spurs in the League Cup on the Tuesday after. So they got to see me play at White Hart Lane. Which was a true highlight of mine.

BORO 4 – 0 SHREWSBURY TOWN
AYRESOME PARK, SATURDAY OCTOBER 23RD 1983
PETER FROM LINTHORPE

I was born in 1975, and lived on York Road, facing the back of the fire station. We had lots of family on the road and directly opposite us lived my auntie, uncle and my two cousins.

One of my cousins is the same age as me and the other is about four or five years older. I was eight years old and truth be known I was a Liverpool fan. Growing up in the 80s it was Rush and Dalglish I wanted to emulate on the school playground like every other kid at the time. My prize possessions were my Puma Dalglish 'silvers' trainers that I was kicking around with.

It was Saturday 23rd October 1983 and I was out the front playing Kirby with my cousin when my dad walked out of our house into my aunt and unc's. A minute or so later my dad, uncle and older cousin come out of the house, shouting my other cousin it was time to go to the match, You see, they were all die hard Boro fans and watched the Boro every week. Me, on the other hand, had never been to any live football match and my extensive knowledge of football was the one match a week on the BBC usually being Liverpool or Manchester Utd.

Anyway, as I was stood there, bouncing the ball, with the impeding feeling of having no one to play with, I knowingly asked my dad where they were going.

"Boro match, son," was the reply from my dad.

"Can I come?" I asked.

"No, you're a Liverpool fan," was his reply.

So, head down and slowly walking back to my house bouncing the ball, I heard them from afar shouting, "Come on, hurry up then." They were waiting on the corner so I quickly booted my ball over our back fence and ran down to catch them up.

To get from our house to the match we went through the alleys of Linthorpe back of Cumberland Road. As we got to the village, the three of us got some money to go into the shop to get some pop and sweets while my dad and uncle had the quickest pint or two in history. I got some cola cubes to eat at the match.

We were finally at Ayresome Park and we were playing Shrewsbury Town. I have to be honest, I had not heard of them or any of the players and was starting to think to myself why did I come here? Anyway, we entered the ground and went to the far end of the Holgate near the seats where my dad and uncle used to chat to some of their friends who used to sit in the seats.

Eventually it was time for kick off and we won 4 nil. The atmosphere absolutely gripped me that day and I literally could not wait for the next home match. Needless to say my Liverpool duvet set and my 'Match' pictures of Nicol, Dalglish, Rush and co were quickly removed from my bedroom and replaced with a Boro squad picture and a badge pinned to my curtains and I've remained a Boro fan for my sins ever since. So moral of the story is I blame my dad and have never forgiven him.

BORO 2 – 1 ASTON VILLA
AYRESOME PARK, APRIL 3RD 1954
PETER HODGSON

As far as I can recall, as this goes a LONG WAY back, my first adventure to the 'hallowed ground' known as Ayresome Park was in April 1954, just before my eighth birthday.

Back then I lived in Milbank Street, which was on what is now known as Cannon Park and our street was opposite Leaders Wood shop near the old infirmary.

My dad's mate Stuart was a footie fan and played for Erimus R.A. in the old Wednesday afternoon league. Yet my dad NEVER watched a football game in his life.

Stuart said to me one day, "I'm going to the match tomorrow – would you like to go?"

What? I ran to mam and dad and asked, begged, pleaded to be allowed to go – and of course they said yes.

So a couple of days later, April 3rd 1954, Stuart called for me after lunch and with his son, Jimmy, we set off up Fleetham Street and up through the little maze of streets until we ended up walking up Warwick Street and out onto Ayresome Street – and there it was – Ayresome Park.

It seemed MASSIVE.

We walked around most of the ground for a quick look at what was going on and I recall how it was so busy – where would all these people go – would they all fit in? We went into a turnstile – never been in one of these before so me and Jimmy are squeezed into a space big enough for only one of us but out we popped and we were inside the ground – followed seconds later by Stuart.

(I now realise that this was 'my first ever squeeze' at a footie match. I had plenty more in the next few years).

We followed Stuart up the concrete stairs into a place called the Boys End and Stuart disappeared. We went to the far end of the Boys End to wait for him. All I could see right then was a HUGE footie pitch – bright green grass, brilliant white lines and goalie nets. Amazing. Fabulous.

Minutes later Stuart arrived and lifted us both over the concrete wall into this huge mass of people (the East End). We walked down to the front, almost onto the pitch, and stopped at the path round the ground. Stuart said we could go and stand next to the wall at the front behind the goalie and he would be stood just behind us on the steps.

I was overwhelmed by how many people were coming into the ground and then my whole body shook as they all cheered and jumped up and down and waved their arms about – and the BORO – resplendent in red and white strip ran onto the pitch, kicking a ball into the net as they practised for a few minutes. Then the other team came out and people booed them. What was that for? They were called Aston Villa and I did like their shirts in maroon with sky blue sleeves.

Kick-off 3pm and the ref's whistle got the game going. It was amazing. The speed of the players, tackles and men sliding all over, the roar of the crowd and then – a goal – and another – and another – flipping heck – this was great! There was so much going on.

It seemed like it was all at 100 miles an hour. I had never seen anything like it before. It was a spectacle I had never imagined. The Boro scored two goals and I thought my ears would burst at the noise – I recall jumping up and down with Jimmy – oh the others scored one but who cared – we WON 2-1.

What a carry on at the end of the game. It was packed trying to get out through the crowd but everyone was happy and smiling. We made it back to Milbank Street and Stuart stopped at Rea's ice cream shop and bought us an ice cream wafer sandwich. Rea's was just the best ice cream ever and a great way to celebrate a Boro win. Stuart had pointed out to me a few of the better known players – the most famous was Wilf Mannion – who I had heard mentioned before – and two other favourites of mine over the next few years. Lindy Delapenha – a speedy West Indian outside right – and a tall, elegant Welshman name of Bill Harris who I saw many times afterwards. I just loved watching Bill play.

I was also pleased to get their autographs when I started to go more regularly over the next two years.

That first day was the April 3rd 1954. I next went a couple of weeks later on Easter weekend against Sunderland with Stuart and Jimmy and we stood in the Boys End that game as it was absolutely packed and he thought we would be safer – almost 39,000 people. To be honest, it was a bit scary. It was a 0-0 draw. Not happy at all with that score but it was an exciting game and the crowd was amazing. Boro got relegated that season. I didn't really realise the enormity of that fact.

In August 1954 I missed the first couple of games in season 1954/55 as I was on holiday at my aunty's farm but Boro were losing games all the time – eight losses in a row and so my next game attended was against West Ham United from London. I wanted to go to that game because they also played in maroon and sky blue – same as Aston VANILLA. (You know like kids call clubs and things daft little names – well I still call Aston Villa – Aston VANILLA!) and I also 'follow' Burnley FC and Scunthorpe FC who both wear the claret and blue.

My trip to see West Ham was on October 30th 1954 and we beat West Ham by 6-0. Yippee!! New signing Charlie Wayman scored four for Boro that day. He had been signed by Boro boss, Bob Dennison for £8,000 from Preston a couple of weeks earlier to help stop all the losses and he failed to hit the net in his first five games but made up for it by notching 4 against West Ham. Everyone thought we'd turned the corner!

Saturday 6th November. We 'turned up and played' against Blackburn Rovers at Ewood

Park looking to shake the Rovers up after our 6-0 win. Hmmm?

There were no radio reports back then, so like many people we did not get to know the scores until the Sports Gazette came out about 5.45pm. I stood outside the newsagents on Cannon Street opposite the Western Club till the Gazette van delivered the rolled-up bundle of Sports Gazettes. As we all opened our copies – gasps of horror – we had LOST – been murdered 9 goals to nil. Numb! Shocked!

Still our worst ever away defeat!!

It was 50 yards back to number 110 Milbank Street – I cried all the way home. Hey, I was only eight.

That was it. Truly I was never going to go again. But I did – probably approaching about 1,700 games with Boro by now and another couple of hundred internationals, Cup Ties and Finals, two World Cup tournaments and two Euro Nations means I could be heading for 2,000 games in the next couple of years.

So here we are, 66 – yes SIXTY SIX years of travelling and watching later and I still kick the cat when we lose and I still feel on top of the world when we win.

I've had some amazing times with fans throughout the years and got to know many players over the last fifty years and have enjoyed just about every season – apart from 1985/86 – but 1986/87 and ever since then made up for it. So I remember many friends who are no longer with us who watched for all their lives and were not as lucky as folk of my generation have been. Long may it continue.

UP the BORO

BORO 6 – 2 QPR
AYRESOME PARK, SEPTEMBER 26TH 1970
PETER MACKIN

One of my earliest Ayresome Park memories is from September 26th 1970. Arriving a few minutes late for the Division Two League match v QPR, we were advised by the gateman the Boro were already 2-0 down. My dad wondered if we should instead go and watch my Uncle Laurence who played Saturday League for Shell Teesport, but decided to stick with the lads. We were rewarded with a stunning 6-2 win, a hat trick for big John Hickton, two for Hugh McIlmoyle and one for Derrick Downing, in front of a crowd of 16,788. Happy days.

BORO 2 – 2 CHARLTON
AYRESOME PARK, MARCH 25TH 1972, ATT 11,100
PHIL CAREY

The first time I went to Ayresome Park was with my dad in August 1971 to see Benfica in a 1-1 friendly. I had just turned seven and my lasting memory is of my dad eulogising about Eusebio and then him laughing out loud when Nobby Stiles clattered him.

It wasn't until March 1972 that I made my full debut at a competitive game at Ayresome Park against the less distinguished opposition of Charlton Athletic. I was taken by Adrian Luke along with two of his sons Nick and Anthony. The game finished 2-2 after Boro had been leading 2-0, Hickton and McMordie scored for the Boro.

We finished 9th on 46 points and Charlton

were relegated. We sat in the East Stand. I think there must have been some offer on as another mediocre season came to an end. But we were hooked and the following season I became a regular in the Boys End and it was from there I saw pretty much the same group of players' storm the league in 1973/74. Happy Days.

BORO 2 – 0 SPURS
AYRESOME PARK, SATURDAY FEBRUARY 5TH 1977
PHILIP TALLENTIRE

It happened forty three years ago but I can remember it like yesterday.

My first ever live game was Middlesbrough versus Tottenham at Ayresome Park on Saturday, February 5th 1977.

Spurs were struggling in Division One and would eventually go down while Boro were still under the canny stewardship of Jack Charlton. Despite having three brothers and a sister, I grew up in a household that had pretty much zero interest in the sport and was indoctrinated by school friends, including my next door neighbour Richard Beadle, who was a big Boro fan. His dad George and his uncle Phil were talented sportsmen and also supported Boro and they, from time-to-time would let me go to games with them at Ayresome Park. Both have sadly passed away but I'll be forever grateful for their kindness.

The day of my first game exists as snapshots. It was a crisp, cold, sunny winter's afternoon. The 32 mile journey from our farm in Teesdale passed more quickly than I expected and, on the way, I can recall passing Feethams as we drove through Darlington – this was pre-bypass days. It was my first visit to Teesside and landmarks like Stockton Racecourse and the number of floodlights on the land opposite what is now Teesside Park. Industrial Middlesbrough was a huge culture shock to a country bumpkin like me.

We parked on the side streets off West Lane and walked to the ground via the red footbridges that cross the A66. Being a sweet tooth, I noted the shop on Acklam Road and would call in many times in future visits.

My first view of the pitch was from the back of the Holgate having walked up the steep

steps at the back of the stand. And, yes, the vivid green of the surface made a memorable impact.

Myself and Richard watched the game sitting on the wall to the left of the goal and I know I was slightly intimidated by the 'townie'

238

kids! That feeling wasn't helped when a fan was dragged out of the crowd to our left with blood streaming from a head wound and marched away by a squad of Bobbies.

The narrowness of the goal stanchion stood out, as did its closeness to the Holgate. The game passed in a blur. Both goals of a 2-0 win were scored at the opposite end of the ground so it was hard to make out what happened other than that David Mills got both. Fortunately, the Tyne Tees cameras were at the game and I could watch the highlights, including the two goals, the following afternoon on Shoot. I even managed to identify myself and my desperately uncool parka when the cameras lingered on the Holgate End.

I was hooked.

BORO 0 – 2 OLDHAM
AYRESOME PARK, LEAGUE DIVISION 3, SATURDAY SEPTEMBER 10TH 1966
RAY DALES

I guess like a lot of young couples in the 50s, my mum and dad had a routine on a Saturday when they were courting (as I believe the term was then!). They lived in Brotton and would get the United bus into town, go to the match together, have something to eat afterwards, and then get the bus back. This continued until I appeared in late 1959, and they then stopped going.

In the 1960s, my dad was Blast Furnace Manager at Skinningrove Iron Works as it was then. (As an aside, if he had to go in on a Saturday morning for whatever reason, he sometimes used to take me with him, leave me with the guys in the shunting yard, and they'd let me ride on the trains with them as they shunted wagons around until my dad had finished – can you imagine that now!)

Anyway, through work he was given tickets for the World Cup games at Ayresome… and yes, he was there for the North Korea match. From one of the matches he brought me back the World Cup Programme (still got it) and I remember being fascinated with everything about it.

I don't actually remember asking to go to Boro, but years later my mum told me that one Saturday early in the new season after the World Cup, my dad said to her, "I think I'll take the lad to the match – see if he likes it…" so I was an excuse for him to go again. I was six.

I remember very little of the day but the bits I do remember are vivid:

- we drove there in my dad's cherry red and white Triumph Herald, the registration number of which was CYG 998B!

- we went with my uncle and cousin.

- we sat in the lower part of the North Stand half way between the tunnel and the East Stand.

- I had a Mars Bar (why do I remember that?).

- Oldham played in blue and white striped shirts and white shorts.

- we lost 0-2 (the first of many disappointments, but at least it was ingrained early).

…and I was absolutely hooked.

Because of the wonders of the internet, I can now see that I was one of 8,932 there that day and the team was Des McPartland, Billy Horner,

Gordon Jones, Bill Gates, Dickie Rooks, David Chadwick, Eric McMordie, Ian Davidson, Jim Irvine, John O'Rourke, and Bobby Braithwaite – Geoff Butler came on for John O'Rourke. I can honestly say I have absolutely no recollection of Davidson or Braithwaite at all – the names don't even ring a bell.

We went to nearly all the rest of the games that season, and I remember crying my eyes out because I wasn't allowed to go the Oxford match to see us get promotion because it was a night match. I also remember fairly early on that season, my dad had to go away for a fortnight with work (to Mauritania, a big iron ore producing country then – might still be now, no idea) and my mum took me to a match and we queued up after and got Geoff Butler's autograph – the things you remember!

One final thing – I have no idea what happened to my collection of programmes from those early years, because I kept them religiously, and wrote my match reports on them – probably chucked by my mum when I left for Uni or something. Anyway, fifty and a bit years later, I opened a present from my

wife and kids on my birthday and inside was a programme from that Boro v Oldham match in pristine condition – god knows how they'd tracked one down, but it now has pride of place next to my 1966 World Cup programme.

I should add that thirty odd years after my dad got me hooked into the Boro before I had any choice in the matter, I did exactly the same with my son and daughter. They were both four when I first took them. They're now twenty two and thirteen respectively, and as mad about the Boro as I am, if not more so!

BORO 2 – 0 LIVERPOOL
AYRESOME PARK, OCTOBER 7TH 1961
RICHARD PIERS RAYNER

Right, this is how it was. My paternal grandparents had bought their house in Tavistock Street in Middlesbrough for one compelling reason: it was just a few doors away from Ayresome Park. The old ground loomed up at the end of the street with those little hutches that, on matchdays, opened onto the turnstiles that, in turn, once you'd managed their stiff, creaking resistance allowed you access to the South Terrace or the upper tier of the South Stand where wooden bench seating was your reward for forking out a few extra pennies.

So, the edifice was imprinted on my imagination from an early age. If it was a match day, a family visit to grandma and grandad's house was an intriguing experience and, as a small boy, I started to wonder what it was all about. For a start there was the herring bone parking of the cars that allowed maximum use of limited space. I'd be in the front room when those car doors started banging and the sound of trampling feet on the cobblestones outside echoed louder and louder as the traffic increased and the crowd started to build up.

In the winter there were only two reasons that you'd go out into the backyard at Tavistock Street: one was to get a shovel of coal for the fire in the parlour and the other was to use the outdoor loo. (I can still smell the paraffin lamp that lit the freezing little cubicle and feel the unwelcome scratch of the Izal toilet paper on my unmentionables). But, if it was a matchday there was an added bonus... you could hear the music of the oompah band that used to march up and down the pitch as part of the pre-match entertainment and even, better, if it was a gloomy afternoon, the floodlights would be on, illuminating the smoky air. Then, when the game was underway, you'd hear the crowd, rousing cheers, groans of despair and the thunder of feet stamping the wooden boards of the grandstand as the excitement built up. It was irresistibly enticing.

But there were further mysteries. Grandad, muffled up against the cold, would join the throng as kick-off time approached, setting off in good spirits, but it didn't last and his mood had changed for the worst by 5 o'clock and he returned home, entering the house with a blast of winter chill and the heady aroma of tobacco smoke. Grandma would be sitting by the fire, diligently writing down the football results as they came over the radio so they could check their pools coupon later on. "What a load of rubbish!" grandad would announce. "That's the last time I'm going there!" And he'd sit fuming as tea was served, his mood hardly improved by the fact that grandma had got one or two results wrong or had only heard one team's score, so you'd get something like 'Manchester City 2 Leicester City…?' (The later invention of the teleprinter really was a boon to mankind).

Nevertheless, another matchday would roll around and the same ritual would be repeated, the build up of the crowd, the low rumble of voices, the brass band playing, the floodlights blazing. It would get to a quarter to three and grandad would be surreptitiously getting into his overcoat. "Where do you think you're going?" asked grandma. "Because I'm sure I heard you say you were never going to set foot in Ayresome Park again as long as you lived." But grandad was already halfway out of the door about to disappear among the bustling shapes jostling their way along the pavement, his last words hanging in the air, "I'm going to give them one more chance!"

For the record, my first game was on October 7th 1961. Boro v Liverpool in the old Second Division. I'd become increasingly intrigued by the matchday ritual and had become an avid reader of the sports pages in the newspapers and had been pleading to be allowed to go to a game since some time in the late 50s, invariably being told to wait until I was older although grandad was slightly more encouraging (if that's what you call it) when he told my father, "We've both suffered long enough on Saturday afternoons… it's about time he had a turn."

In the end we all went together. Grandad, dad and me, three generations of the family off to see the Boro. And all the clichés were true. We had seats in the South Stand, the turnstiles made that clunky sort of reluctant grinding sound as we entered before we climbed the gloomy rickety stairs and there was a smell of damp among the combined whiff of woodbines, pipe smoke and stale Newboulds pies. And then we emerged into the light. The pitch spread out before us, green and bright under the floodlights, the marching band was there and the ground was alive with noise and expectation. To my right, the vast open space of the uncovered East End rose up towards the little concrete box where the half time scoreboard was located. On the left the Holgate End looked busy and bustling although it would be a few years before it became a real focus for the ground's most vocal supporters. And in front of us was the main grandstand in all its Edwardian splendour. Seats in the upper tier for the posh folk and below that the option to stand and end up frozen to one of the metal barriers along the North Terrace, roughly in the middle of which was the players' tunnel.

Seeing the pitch for the first time like that is one of those moments the magic of which still endures. I don't remember much of the game itself. Liverpool were on their way to promotion under Bill Shankly and an era of unprecedented success awaited them but this was Boro's afternoon. It was 0-0 at half-time and in my naiveté I thought that was it and might even have been a bit disappointed to be told we had another 45 minutes to get through when the warm fireside seemed a much better option. But it all came good in the end and Boro won 2-0, both own goals courtesy of a Liverpool player called White. Later on that evening, when I'd thawed out, I realised that I'd enjoyed myself enormously. The mysteries had started to reveal themselves!

SHOULD'VE BROUGHT A BRICK...
AYRESOME PARK
RITA LOCKE

All you want is the date, time, result and who was playing and not a lot of extraneous material. I cannot promise that. I cannot give you the date but I was about sixteen or seventeen years old. I had been wanting to go to Ayresome Park for years but my parents would not allow me to go. (Bad Language).

I persuaded my brother in law to take me eventually. We caught one of the special buses that left North Ormesby market place for Linthorpe Road, as did the bus-loads of fellas coming from South Bank, Grangetown on the trackless and dropped off in North Ormesby. Reaching Ayresome Park we squeezed through the turnstile and went to the Bob End, onto the terracing and got a place behind a suitable crush barrier. So this was it – a great sight for me – an expanse of green grass as big as a football pitch and an impressive looking stadium which was slowly filling up. Very exciting. There was a brass band playing near the corner flag. Most people seemed to ignore it but politely clapped when they finished.

The area where we were standing was becoming crowded and although not small for a female (I am just over 5ft 3in), I can't be certain but I am almost sure there were some remarks like, "Should've brought a brick." Whether true or not, apparently some people had on occasion brought a brick to stand on – I don't know. All lies, I'm sure!

I saw the football match and, yes, it was

exciting in spite of the fact that my view was somewhat obstructed. The atmosphere was terrific. Lots of noise, oohs ahs, the insults to the ref, the cheers, the strong language, occasionally. I saw some of the match and some of the players. I was happy when we left so perhaps we won. We had something special we had watched our team play footie. And we were all in it together. Who we played I can't remember now. Who played in the team, I can't remember now but it was pre-Clough in the first team. After that, I went to see the Boro play with my friend Pat, not in the Bob End but usually along the side of the Marske (Machine Company) Stand. Later, there was Clough who scored so many goals. Of course with the forward line of Day, McClean, Clough, Peacock and Holliday, the goals were guaranteed. Cup Finals and promotion beckoned. Such is hope! It took a long time. We will of course not be relegated this season but if we are what can you do? It's the BORO.

BORO 1 – 0 ARSENAL
AYRESOME PARK, APRIL 6TH 1993
ROB FLETCHER, BORO MAG

The first live football match I ever saw was against George Graham's Arsenal. At this point, I'd seen bits of football on TV – mainly my uncle's videos of Gazza at Tottenham, but never seen one live. After getting tickets from a family friend, I travelled to the game with my dad. It was the first of many games we would watch together.

The main memory I had, as an eight year old, was the lack of commentary in the stadium. I was surprised when the game started that no one was telling me who the players were or what I should be looking out for. Once I'd got over that, the view we had was high if I remember, and I felt like the floodlights brought the match to life.

Any memory of the match is pretty much wiped now but I do remember noting down the line ups and John Hendrie's winner.

So I suppose the lasting memory of my first game was that the fan's voice was the most important inside a football ground.

BORO 1 – 0 OXFORD UNITED
AYRESOME PARK, LEAGUE DIVISION TWO, DECEMBER 30TH 1972
ROJOR

I would love to claim my first match was a glamorous topflight encounter with Ayresome Park packed to the rafters and the pitch littered with international superstars, but it was not. I was eight years old and I was frozen to the bone. My mother had hastily knitted me a red and white scarf, but it offered only token protection from the icy cold December wind. My father was a somewhat cynical Boro fan in the long-held Teesside tradition and warned me young that, "The Boro always let you down." I was prepared for a lifetime of footballing heartache from day one. Armed with a flask of soup, I got a squeeze (Teesside parlance for 'free' entry by squeezing through the turnstile with your dad) and we stood on the Holgate. Being Christmas time, the floodlights were on and the smell of cigars hung in the air – even to this day that smell reminds me of those terraces. I was one of only 9,069 fans that Saturday and our hero turned out to be

Alan Foggon in a 1-0 victory over the mighty Oxford United. I cannot remember any of the match only the frostbite, but the die was cast, and I had been bitten by the bug – Come on BORO!

SQUEEZE
AYRESOME PARK
BY SCOTT TURNBULL AGED NINE AND THREE QUARTERS

I'm nine… and three quarters. I'm queuing outside Ayresome Park for the last game of the season. I'm wearing my Puma Spectrum tracksuit with the green and blue Dickens top underneath. I have my precious ticket clasped tightly in my tiny, pink hand. Behind me is Graham Bell's dad. "Don't worry, Scotty," he says to me through wonky, nicotine-stained teeth, "stay close." I do as I'm told. I mean, I'm only nine and three quarters.

We're doing a 'squeeze'. I heard everyone talking about it at the pub earlier, but I'm still slightly confused. Nobody seems to have run the whole concept past me. That's probably because I spend the majority of my time

thinking about transformers and Scalextric –
and who could blame me, I'm nine and three
quarters!

But between you and me, I'm a little bit
scared. As we get closer and closer to the
front of the queue, I start thinking – what is a
squeeze? What's getting squeezed? And most
importantly, who's getting squeezed?

Finally, we get to the turn-style. Graham's
dad proffers the young lad behind the counter
a fresh 20 and winks. The lad winks back.
What's going on now, I think? Why's everyone
winking? Everybody seems to know what's
going on except me! This seems slightly unfair
cause I'm only nine and three quarters!

And that's when it happens – Graham's
dad takes me by the shoulders and pushes me
forwards into the turnstile. And in my head,
I'm shouting – 'What are you doing, you mad
old b'stard???' For what seems like an eternity,
the two of us are closer than beans on toast,
crammed into the tiny space in the miniature
metal roundabout, shuffling towards the
promised land...

...On the other side it's like a carnival: I've

never seen so many people, red and white everywhere. At that moment, there's nowhere else I'd rather be. And in my head, I think being a Boro fan is the best feeling in the world. But of course, I don't know any better. I'm only nine and three quarters…

BORO 1 – 0 LIVERPOOL
AYRESOME PARK, MAY 6TH 1980
SHAUN WILSON

I was always football mad as a kid growing up in East Cleveland, but it wasn't a Boro player who was my first hero. That was Liverpool's Kenny Dalglish, and I flirted with being a fan of the Merseyside team. That all changed on May 6th 1980, Boro's penultimate game of the 1979/80 season. My Uncle Eric took me to Ayresome Park aged eight to watch Boro take on league leaders Liverpool. I remember it was a night match, which seemed to take on extra mystical powers. We sat in the South Stand Upper, near to the away fans. I can remember the smell of the pies and the Bovril. Like everyone says, the vivid green hue of the Ayresome pitch, and the barrelled roof of the North Stand opposite. The game itself saw David Shearer score the winner for Boro in a 1-0 win, and then days later we beat Arsenal 5-0 (which I didn't attend). I was hooked, and Boro were my team from then on in, as I thought world domination was imminent. We got relegated two years later.

BORO 1 – 1 LIVERPOOL
AYRESOME PARK, 1977
SIMON BOLTON

My dad took me to my first game aged nine at the start of the 1977/78 season when Boro played Liverpool. I think Souness was making his first return as we stood in the Holgate and a few girls near us kept shouting, "Love you, Graeme!" I remember just how noisy it seemed and the loudness of the singing, so much different to the TV. We drew 1-1 so not a bad result. It was actually eleven years later before I went to my first away game, the opening game of the 88/89 season back in Div One at Derby. Sadly we lost 1-0 but I went to most away games that season so it didn't put me off.

THINKING THIS IS A BIT MAD...
AYRESOME PARK
SIMON CLIFFORD

Not really strong memories but I was told I went to a reserves game when I was four or five. They said it was against Arsenal but I don't know if it could have been because I don't know if we played Arsenal in reserve games. But I hadn't liked it maybe because of the crowd. So, four or five, it would have been 74 or 75 season.

I started going properly with Michael my next door neighbour above where the players came out into the posh seats, next to the Hundred Club. We weren't in that but he had a Season Ticket and took me to every match. My first memories are of being up there. Maybe I started going in the last season of Jack Charlton but I was definitely there for the beginning of John Neal. Hazy memories of John Neal against Liverpool and a draw. Thinking this is a bit mad. I realised Liverpool were the top team. Or a top team. And we had competed with them. I remember I didn't think that would happen. And also that season

I remember watching Craig Johnston warm up and someone said to me this is the young Aussie kid and we were watching him from behind where he warmed up on a night match and I have never seen anyone warm up for as long. In fact I had never seen anyone warm up on the side, he was doing loads of things with his hips. I wouldn't say it was impressive but it was a bit different.

A match that stands out that season is probably playing Everton. It was a close game in the FA Cup and we had beaten Coventry 3-0 in one of the earlier rounds. And after beating Everton I was thinking wow we could win the FA Cup. I was always fascinated by these big city teams you saw on TV when they came to Middlesbrough that we could get anything against them. It made me start to think in life you can take on the big boys. Anything is possible. It became a fascination for me. Obviously Man Utd used to come and maybe the best we could get was a draw at odd times.

Then came Orient and the first time I had seen Ayresome Park full and what a magical day. In my head I thought we are going to go on and win the FA Cup and of course we didn't even beat Orient.

It reminded me of Leicester City end of season game under Bruce Rioch, party, carnival atmosphere and it goes flat.

BORO V SHEFFIELD WEDNESDAY
AYRESOME PARK, NOVEMBER 25TH 1988
JAMES STANWAY

The first ever issue of fmttm was November 25th 1988 against Sheffield Wednesday. That also was my first ever Boro match. We lost that day. Boro were just merely setting me up for the rest of my footballing life. No one ever forgets their first game. I didn't want to go as it was cold but my dad insisted we go. I remember thinking I would be bored so I even took my Beano comics with me. I even remember seeing someone with a footballing comic, little did I realise it was the first issue of fmttm and the irony is that one day I would be regularly contributing my thoughts on Boro to the fanzine.

I never did read those Beanos.

WE WERE ABSOLUTELY CLASS AT HOME...
STE ALLEN

My first game was away to Newcastle 90/91 but I prefer to keep that one buried away because my dad sold me out so that he could get corporate seats. He'd told me I could go and that I'd be mascot... he didn't mention which team I was mascot for until we got to St James' Park. I remember meeting Colin Todd, Tony Mowbray and Bernie Slaven and telling them I was a Boro supporter immediately. The most impressive thing was seeing a scale model of the plans for St James' Park. It looked exactly like it did for the season that they choked on that 12 point lead!

The game was awful. Nil nil. One of my dad's mates won the match ball in a raffle.

My first game at Ayresome was Millwall – opening day of 91/92. Lennie's first game in charge and Mustoe scored on his debut. We were sat in the North Stand just to the left of the half way line probably about four or five rows back – we sat there or thereabouts at nearly every home game for the next two seasons before I moved to the East and then eventually the Holgate for the final season there.

My memory from the game is blurry but I remember the goal, Ripley cutting inside and threading a ball through... then a mass of bodies seemingly shrouded the ball, everyone around us stood up and I couldn't see a thing. I think my dad must've pulled me up or lifted me just in time for me to see the ball as it passed their keeper and nestled in the bottom corner. I remember going absolutely daft because I'd never seen a goal before but more than that, the whole thing just felt like complete chaos. We'd scored, I'd only just barely seen it go in and I didn't have a clue who scored it but I did not give a sh*t about any of that! I definitely thought it was Mark Proctor for the next twenty years before I saw the highlights from the match on YouTube twenty years later. But Mustoe became one of my all time favourite Boro players and scored an absolute screamer against Watford in 94/95 which I DEFINITELY knew was his and I think that's my favourite goal I've ever seen live.

That's about the extent of what I remember from my first game at Ayresome. I have more collective memories of that season because we were absolutely class at home so I was spoilt rotten. It took five games for anyone to even score past us at Ayresome (Sunderland) and we were undefeated until Portsmouth knocked us out of the Cup in a Round 5 replay when I think Willie Falconer ended up playing at left back.

Oh and back to the Newcastle match, and the match ball that was won got ruined in the car park afterwards as everyone was playing with it.

BORO 6 – 2 QPR
AYRESOME PARK, SEPTEMBER 26TH 1970
STEPHEN HARRISON (UNCLE HARRY)

I was ten years and three days old. From the front wall of the Chicken Run, me and our kid gazed upon the glamorous fancy dannery of QPR. Marsh, Clement and Venables and their elaborate hoopy get up. Five minutes gone, we were 2 nil down. One of us went to the privvy, McIlmoyle scores. We felt the two events were mystically linked so the other one went – McIlmoyle scored again. We now gleefully knew some magick was at play and continued our winning streak. The game become famous for Hughie's dazzling display, as well as Downing's goal and Hickton's hatrick that humbled the hoops. We take nothing away from our heroes that day but we knew then and know now that we played our part via the unfathomable connection between fans, footballers and the Chicken Run urinals. UTB

BORO 1 – 1 BENFICA
AYRESOME PARK, 1971
STEVE CHESTER

I was nine years of age and my dad took me to watch the mighty Boro play Benfica (who were on a pre-season tour) on a very wet August evening 1971.

My grandma used to live at No 8 Chester Street, a stone's throw from Ayresome Park and I vividly remember departing from there and heading to the game. We had seats up in the North Stand and probably the only time I ever had a seat at Ayresome Park as from that day forward I was generally always in the Bob End.

I remember thinking how green the pitch was, it reminded me of a snooker table, and how excited I was to see Eusebio play. Hickton gave us the lead from a Johnny Vincent cross but Benfica pulled one back (Eusebio left the field injured) and the game ended up 1-1. It wasn't the greatest of games but for a nine year old it was a fantastic night. I only found out today (forty nine years later) that Benfica were managed by Jimmy Hagan that night who was from county Durham!

Note... My first ever league game was at home to Leyton Orient not long afterwards and I will always remember waiting outside near the famous Middlesbrough FC 'gates', autograph book in hand and my dad saying, "See that guy over there, son, leaning against that post/wall smoking a ciggy...? well that's Willy Whigham." I was in awe! Hahaha

Boro – Willie Whigham, Mike Allen, Gordon Jones, Nobby Stiles (Eric McMordie 80), Stuart

Boam, Frank Spraggon, Derrick Downing, David Mills, John Hickton, Johnny Vincent, Joe Laidlaw.

BORO V GRIMSBY TOWN
AYRESOME PARK, 1962/63
DR STEVE SHERLOCK

When I was first asked by Rob Nichols to write this, I thought – well, this will be easy, because as a Boro fan 'through and through', I well remembered my first match. However, as an archaeologist (it's a dirty job but someone has to do it), I should have realised how shaped we are by our past and how memory and recollections are so important. Please remember that bit.

So, I knew it was against Grimsby Town and I knew it was in 1962/3 and that I went from Marske with my grandad, that we went in the South Stand and I got a squeeze through the turnstiles (ask yer dad!). All of that has proven to be correct.

The next bit of detail… I had confidently said, "It was a 1-1 draw." Jim Irvine equalised and Gordon Jones played at Left Back. Only one out of three correct there, being right about Gordon Jones, Boro's 700+ appearance left back, who one season in the 1960s played fifty games for the Boro – what an achievement. Anyroad (sic) this is the important bit… I remembered Grimsby scoring and someone twirling their rattle (back to yer dad for that one as well, I am afraid) and the chant going up "bring out the equaliser…" (never heard of it).

This is the important lesson, the Boro lost and I completely forgot about that – or selectively edited it in my memory, as I had become a Boro fan and we don't dwell on our defeats, do we now? As I write this, I can recall days later reading and re-reading the football programme with a pink cover but only text, league table, fixtures. Clearly there were no fun things like Donkey Watch, it was a serious business being a Boro fan in the 1960s!

So what can we learn from the past? Remember I am an archaeologist – this is an open goal even Alves couldn't miss… I became a lifelong Boro fan, no matter what, rarely watch other matches (they seem meaningless) and if they lose, forget that and look forward to the next match. The second lesson (excuse me here) is as I said to my son, "You can pick your nose, but you cannot pick your football team." So when we lived outside the Boro, and he had been indoctrinated as a Boro fan, he no doubt had interesting playground experiences with all of the Leeds and Man U fins (sic). However, that's his story not mine… was I a bad dad and did I take him to his first defeat… Well, I will let him tell you that…

BURY V BORO
RIVERSIDE STADIUM, 1997/98
DR JAKE SHERLOCK

I remember parts of my first Middlesbrough game clearer than others. I believe I was six or seven years old, making it around the 97/98 season. I remember clearly going with my dad to an away game and I think it was at Bury. I remember getting a train to and from the match and have a feeling that we won. I'm unsure as to what the final score was or who scored. I'm sure it wasn't Juninho, had it been a Juninho goal I'm sure I would have remembered that. Now, obviously I was always Middlesbrough to my core, that was never in question, however thinking about it now it's somewhat of a gamble taking your child to an away game for their first match. A bewildering environment to begin with you then take your small impressionable child and surround them with Bury fans. Had it been a different result, say a 3-0 Bury win, a lesser young fan could have been tempted by glory and the gleaming lights Bury had to offer. You could have unintentionally taken home a Bury fan. Fortunately my resolve was strong, I grew up wanting to be Roary the Lion, that is until one evening Ravanelli passed us on the dual carriageway in his silver Ferrari and I decided I wanted to be able to afford his Ferrari (sadly taking being Roary off the table).

I don't so much remember details of the game instead it is the experience of going to a football match for the first time that forms the majority of my memories. I remember the noise and excitement, the shouting and towering crowds around me. I think we were sat in a corner of the stadium to the left of the goal, around half way up and I think we may have been in with the home supporters. I don't remember any goals at our end and I think it was either winter or being played at night as I remember the floodlights being on and it being cold and dark outside when we left. I remember the train after the game, trying to blend in with what were mainly home fans as we travelled back. I also remember a pre and possibly post-match reminder from my dad, reminding me not to repeat any new words or phrases I heard at the match to my mum.

Since being asked to think about my first match and write about it, I believe I have had competing memories contesting in my mind, vying to be remembered as my first match. Another is an away match possibly at Nottingham Forest but I now think this may just be a complete fabrication and perhaps didn't exist at all. My dad will know for sure and I need to ask him, we haven't discussed it so as to preserve my uninfluenced memory. Trying to remember these moments in time from about twenty five years ago is difficult as there isn't quite enough of the memory to form a clear narrative today.

Memory is of course a very malleable concept. Our memories are generally divided into two different types, our episodic memory (things that have happened to you, like attending a football match) and your semantic memory (the sum of your general knowledge accrued throughout your life). We forget things and these holes that develop in our mind's autobiography make us uneasy so our brains simply make things up, patching in a few stray facts from our semantic memory that seem to fit. Some people do this more than others with sufferers of cognitive disease like dementia or alcohol-induced brain damage sometimes provoking a state of continuous 'confabulation' where these fabricated stories fill gaps in memory unconsciously.

Do I just remember my first Boro game being a win as it makes me happier remembering it that way? Did my mind fill a hole with a goal? It is possible but I'm not sure it did. If my memory was to be this kind to me, I wouldn't remember so many of the defeats and goalless draws since then. Regardless of the result that day, that game marked the start of a very special time in my childhood when my dad and I started going to Middlesbrough games together.

Soon after that, perhaps a season or two later, my dad and I got our first Season Tickets and began our weekend match routine. We would drive from York to Redcar, seeing my grandma for lunch, before heading on to Middlesbrough. Listening to the pre-match on Century Radio before parking up the car what seemed like about ten miles from the stadium. We would don our hiking boots for a 'shortcut' across an often very muddy field to an underpass, past one pub, over the railway track, pick up a fmttm and into the stadium. Being at the Riverside are where my proper memories are of going to Middlesbrough matches. The familiar chants, the music played when we scored, those sweet wins and with being a Boro fan, inevitable defeats. I love these memories as there is enough substance to them for me to grasp hold of today. My first Boro game is special to me because of what it started rather than my memory that remains of it.

BORO 2 – 1 CRYSTAL PALACE
AYRESOME PARK, 1988
STEVEN LAW

I was seven years old and got a squeeze in at the turnstiles with my dad. We sat in the South Stand lower. I didn't know who any of the players were but remember Tony Mowbray scoring. I thought we were going to watch England.

BORO 3 – 1 SCUNTHORPE UNITED
AYRESOME PARK, 1960
STU MAC (STUART MACFADZEAN)

It was actually sixty years ago that I went to my first match at Ayresome Park on my ninth birthday. We were at home to the mighty Scunthorpe United. I remember getting the match bus from Stockton baths that dropped us near the ground. I can still picture the thrill of seeing the floodlight pylons and paying my 6d (3p). It seemed we were climbing a mountain to the Boys End, but it was worth it to see the pitch for the first time. We did not stop there long as we climbed over the wall and ended up behind the goal. I remember looking up at the half-time scoreboard, which seemed to tower over the open terrace. Apparently, the match ended up 3-1 with Brian Clough scoring twice. But all I can remember about the match is Scunny hitting the bar. But it was enough to get me hooked for life.

BORO 0 – 2 EVERTON
AYRESOME PARK, OCTOBER 1981
STUART DOWNING

I was almost ten years old when I first set foot in Ayresome Park, in October 1981. I knew dad liked the Boro, by the way he would shout at the radio or telly whenever they were on – a trait I would later inherit. I shared a room with my brother, Nige, and its walls were decorated with the glitzy stars of dirty Leeds. I'm not sure if I ever slept that well with Joe Jordan and Paul Reaney staring down at me each night. Character building, I suppose. Anyway, I didn't follow in his footsteps. I liked Everton – I think it was the blue kit with the Umbro branding down the sleeves and Bob Latchford's beard in the Topical Times Football Annual 1978 that did it.

So I persuaded my dad to take me when the Toffees arrived in town.

He wanted to take me to stand in the Boys End, where his dad had first taken him many years ago. Unfortunately, this was also the away end at the time. This didn't bother me much, seeing as how I wanted to see the team in blue. It didn't bother dad either. He would take me in the away end more than once, including a cup tie against Arsenal which had what could be described as a rather lively atmosphere. This game was uneventful though, as far as I can recall. There weren't many Everton fans there to see their team win 0-2, although I have a very clear memory of being able to see one of their supporter's buttocks quite clearly throughout the game as he sat on the sturdy crush barrier below. It wasn't the kind of thing I was used to in Tollesby.

We left before the end to avoid the rush and when I got home, I filled in marks out of ten for all the players on the back of my programme. Everton's players generally scored about seven, but Boro's brave boys almost all got nines or tens. My fickle head had been turned by Billy Woof and Mick Baxter. I was a Boro fan, for better or (more often) for worse and I've managed to stay that way ever since. And thankfully, Nige eventually saw sense too, joining me, Gary and dad in that shared experience that gives you all something to talk about on a Sunday.

BORO 1 – 1 LEYTON ORIENT
AYRESOME PARK
STUART JOHNSON

Ayresome Park, East End seats with our dad. Be about 1967/68 against Leyton Orient. I know many people say this, but I was shocked by the beauty and greenness of the pitch, having previously only watched it on black and white TV!

Any road, me dad said Dicky Rooks would cost us the game, and so he did, getting skinned for a tap in, but I seem to remember it ended 1-1 – who cares?

BORO 6 – 2 QPR
AYRESOME PARK, 1970
STUART WALLACE

My first legal (non squeeze) was QPR 1970, the big memory was Willie Whigham conceding two goals through his legs, running home to see the tele printer on Grandstand displaying Middlesbrough 6 (SIX) - QPR 2.

IT WAS ONE HELL OF A WALK...
AYRESOME PARK
SUE GARDNER

I was about seven or eight. My dad walked me and our Geoff, three years younger, from Stockton to Ayresome Park. I am afraid I can't remember who we were playing, only that it was packed. I think we won though as the crowd was cheering... sorry, not much help to you, it just stuck in my mind. We did this quite a few other times after this, well, until we complained about the long walk.

I know we went via Stockton Road but sometimes we went Portrack Lane way. I think it depended on dad's mood. He refused to get buses and he didn't have a car then. It was one hell of a walk. We took dad to the Riverside once and he complained that the atmosphere was not as good as Ayresome Park, so he wouldn't go any more.

BORO 5 – 1 YEOVIL
RIVERSIDE STADIUM, TUESDAY AUGUST 26TH 2008
THOMAS BARTLEY

A jewel in an otherwise unpleasant crown of a season. After opening our fatal 2008/09 campaign with one win and one loss, we dismissed a Yeovil side we would find on our Championship fixture list a few years down the line. Among those on the scoresheet were now country and western star Mido (anyone who has seen THAT photo will know what I am on about), Jeremie Aliadiere and then new purchase Marvin Emnes who, because of our mutual recent noticing of the club, I developed a soft spot for. It would somehow get even better with a 2-0 victory over Man City in my next game a couple of months later.

BORO 8 – 0 SHEFFIELD WEDNESDAY
AYRESOME PARK, APRIL 1974
TIM HETHERINGTON

My first Boro game was in April 1974, during the season when Jack Charlton took the club back to the First Division as champions. We were playing Sheffield Wednesday at Ayresome Park and my dad had got an extra ticket... so this was to be the day, a right of passage no less important than others enjoyed across the globe by other six-year olds... "Come on, son... grab your scarf!!" We parked as near to Lappin's typewriter shop as possible, walked to the corner shop for supplies – a quarter of midget gems for me, mint imperials for dad – and made our way to the Warwick Street entrance of the North Stand. I can vaguely remember stopping at the foot of the stairs to visit the 'Gents', effectively a trough full of sheepskin-clad blokes – all making sure that they too wouldn't need to get up out of their seats during the first half, and possibly miss something important. Climbing the big wooden stairs is a memory that will stay with me for ever – seeing the red of the South Stand opposite, and the green of the pitch... a luminescent glow that has never really been bettered in the years since. The rest of the afternoon is a blur – mixed in with 'The Power Game', big Jack collecting tracksuit tops, someone playing the bagpipes for some reason (not sure if that really happened however), Boro winning 8-0 (unbelievably that did actually happen – but I can't recollect any of the goals or goalscorers), and just the general noise which at times felt deafening. I must have walked back to the car after the final whistle with a sense that if that kind of result was going to be repeated every other Saturday then sign me up... who needed Liverpool or Man Utd? – we were league champions and couldn't stop scoring, surely my football-watching future was set.

BORO 3 – 1 SWINDON TOWN
AYRESOME PARK, OCTOBER 29TH 1994
TOM FLIGHT

My first match was at Ayresome Park in October 1994 against Swindon, a couple months into Bryan Robson's revolution. I was seven years old and just starting to get into football. My parents were Londoners and had only moved to the North East in their late 30s. My two older brothers were both Leeds fans at this point, having moved from there a few years earlier. I followed England, and would tape Match of the Day, but Boro was a team I heard everyone talk about yet knew nothing about. I vividly remember not having a connection to them in the same way most of my classmates did. Almost the second I walked out into the stand and saw the pitch, seeing the crowd, feeling the pre-match buzz, a connection was formed with the club that has been unbreakable ever since.

Neil Cox opened the scoring in the opening minutes, marauding into the box to finish off a rapid team move. I still remember the exhilaration of seeing the crowd break into a sea of limbs.

Looking back, October had been a difficult month. We lost at home to title challengers Tranmere, and then got hammered 5-1 away at Luton. This was a return to form, and was a fantastic end-to-end contest, perfect for a young kid witnessing his first match. Jan Fjortoft actually equalised for The Robins and did his signature airplane celebration. Second-half goals from Hendrie and Wilkinson sealed off a feel-good win.

My dad soon became hooked. We went to more games that season, but my brother got dibs on the final game at Luton. By now we were all Boro fans. My dad was one of those who joined the queues to get one of the last Season Tickets when Juninho signed. We had it until I left home ten years later. My memories and experiences as a Boro fan are definitely of the Riverside era, but I'm so pleased I got to experience a match at Ayresome Park.

BORO 2 – 1 WORLD CUP WINNERS WEST HAM
AYRESOME PARK, FA CUP ROUND 3, JANUARY 1970
TONY CLISH

Very vivid memories… An amazing day that changed my life.

Memories play tricks on you over the years and you tend to romanticise, but honestly it's

the first memory of my life that was in strong colour. I had never seen grass so green or shirts so red. We were used to grimy greys everywhere else.

The noise. It was the Ayresome Angel years. The smells – Bovril and cheap cigarettes! It was wonderful. I was hooked!

We won. 2-1. My first sight of John Hickton. Hughie McIlmoyle and Derrick Downing scored.

A wonderful tight squad, managed by the wonderful Stan Anderson.

A Season Ticket for me and my dad from the next season and the build up to the Charlton years had started.

What a journey. I have goosebumps writing this.

Up the Boro (the Boro's going up!)

Unfortunately we didn't follow the 'to stay' in the song lyrics, that would have been far too easy a journey. And watching the Boro for fifty years hasn't been easy, but it has been wonderful!

RIPLEY HAT TRICK SPARKS SPREE
BORO 6 – 0 SHEFFIELD UNITED
AYRESOME PARK, SATURDAY 2ND APRIL 1988
DR TOSH WARWICK

My first Boro game was on Saturday 2nd April 1988 at Ayresome Park. I went to the match as a four-year-old with my dad who I would go to a number of matches at Ayresome with, including the last league match against Luton Town in 1995.

My first match would be a home fixture against struggling Sheffield United. My dad said he couldn't take me in the Holgate End as it was too cold and couldn't get in the Clive Road End so we instead ended up watching the match from the Chicken Run.

I can't remember the match at all... I wish I could as Middlesbrough won 6-0! Boro legend and future England international Stuart Ripley grabbed his first senior hat trick in the match, whilst Trevor Senior scored a brace and Bernie Slaven got the other goal. According to the Evening Gazette match report, sections of the 17,340 crowd were shouting, "We want 10," but Boro had to settle for six. The win left Boro second in the league and the season would ultimately end in promotion to the top flight.

Going along to matches at Ayresome Park as a youngster helped instil a love for Middlesbrough FC that continues to this day as a Season Ticket holder and Boro historian.

Further visits to Boro's old ground with my dad usually included a pre-match visit to The Empire or White Rose and a glass of orange juice and a bag of crisps. Some twenty five years on since the last match at the old ground, I still treasure my memories of Ayresome Park.

A BAPTISM OF FIRE...
RIVERSIDE STADIUM
WILL NETT

Might as well start with a baptism of fire: a Cup Final in 1997. Not that one. Or that one. York City were coming to town to defend the North Riding Senior Cup, previously won by such luminaries as Loftus Albion and Portrack Shamrock, against 45 time winners Middlesbrough in a fervent derby fixture emotionally-charged enough to rival anything in world football. That's how I remember it, anyway, after six pints of pre-match commotion lotion in the Shakespeare pub.

It was a balmy July evening. 'Balmy' of course is how Teessiders describe a cold summer's evening, in an attempt to avoid swearing and say that it was 'f****** freezing'. I can't remember exactly who was on the teamsheet that day, but I'm pretty certain that the All-Stars of the previous season were still on holiday in their respective hometowns, Perugia, Rio and Scunthorpe, to name but three. The 'Minstermen' led by Brian Little, had made the short trip up the A19 for the game, and were as shocked as anyone else in the ground to find themselves 0-1 up inside the first minute. A ball over the top was lobbed neatly over Gary Walsh. I think. The floodlights reflecting off Walsh's bald patch actually impaired my view of what happened from high in the North Stand. Was this a common occurrence, I wondered? I'd never even been inside a football stadium before. I'd peered through the gates of Ayresome Park a week or so after it had closed two years earlier, with the reverence of someone looking into the face of God, but never attended a game there. The 'Cellnet' as it was referred to, was my first experience of the repackaged game I'd heard so much about. I'd been misled on what to expect, it seemed. After half an hour in the ground no one had even p*ssed down the back of my coat.

Boro got themselves back in the game, somehow.

I couldn't see what was happening until Gary Walsh and his bald patch swapped ends at half time. We needed some creativity in the centre of the park, from someone like, say, oh, I don't know… I'll just pull some names out of thin air, Paul Gascoigne, or Paul Merson. I'm told the final score was 3-1. Boro lifted the trophy, at least, and I was ready to usher in an era of watching the club seize cup after cup after cup.

SPURS 0 – 0 BORO
WHITE HART LANE, 2003/04
YUSUF (BORO FAN) JAMA

My first Boro match I attended was an away game at Spurs during the 2003/04 game. It was a very drab 0-0 game and there is not much I can actually remember from the game as I was fairly young at the time. Being based in London, I was always a fan that attended local away games. Only recently I have been able to financially afford and have time to attend matches regularly.

My earliest football memory was Euro 96. I was very young then and can remember the atmosphere in and around Wembley as the tournament was staged in England and all the England games at Wembley. It was my first real buzz of the sport. I didn't really support any football team at this stage. We didn't have a local team to Wembley. All the London clubs were a bit of a distance from where I lived.

All my family and friends supported Man Utd and Liverpool (typical Londoners!) as well as Arsenal and Chelsea. I had no real interest in them. So, the following season after Euro 96 had finished was the 96/97 season and I remember seeing the scoreline and highlights of one particular game that stood out – Middlesbrough 3-3 Liverpool. I remember seeing the Ravanelli celebration and literally just fell in love.

I didn't go to any matches until the 2003/04 season when we had Tottenham away, be that Middlesbrough matches or other football teams. I would support the team from watching on TV. It was great because back in the day we had an unbelievable record against the big boys so we would often win or draw against the likes of Man Utd, Arsenal, Chelsea, Liverpool who all my mates supported, so when we got a great result against them, school on Monday morning was great. They wouldn't take much notice of our defeats to Charlton for example!

As I was only young, I would only be able to go to matches in London on my own. As I got older and could financially afford it, I could stretch it out a bit further. I had a year where I was out of work and a couple of years where I did an apprenticeship so had very limited amount of money, which meant unfortunately I couldn't really go to many, if any, games during this three year period. Fortunately, money got a bit kinder for me and I have been able to attend regularly for the last five years or so now.

I also remember the first visit to the Riverside. Unfortunately this was only in March 2017, and it was always a trek to go there because of how far it was and how much the train tickets were. Anyway, it was the Man City game in the FA Cup Quarter Final and it was a midday kick off, so I was up from about 5am! Anyway, I booked my train tickets to reflect the possibility of extra time, penalties and a bit of time to celebrate full time. As it happens, we were never in the game and got comfortably beaten. But I just remember the first time I walked into the ground, it was brilliant, like a feeling I have never had at any ground I visited. The stadium I have seen for so many years on TV and online – I am finally here.

I was in the West Stand for the game and directly behind the Man City dugout. Singing was difficult for me because nobody around me was really singing, but every away game I went to the fans were always singing and standing. I remember looking to my right and seeing the South Stand in full voice. I have always seen the colourful Red Faction on TV and had huge admiration but my preference has always been to sit lower tier which is why when I decided to move to the South Stand, and I decided to move right by the corner flag so I had a great view. The first time I was there was for the final home game against Southampton where we lost 1-2. Bamford scored his first Premier League goal, Downing got booed when he got subbed off, Guzan got chants of "Off off off," when we conceded a penalty and we sang lots of classic songs from the Karanka era. Very eventful!

VERY FULL AND NOISY...
AYRESOME PARK
YVONNE FERGUSON

I remember going to Ayresome Park with my dad. I was about seven and wore an anorak! Can't remember who we played but my dad held me up in his arms to watch the match. It was so exciting. Full of supporters, very full and noisy. We walked to the car afterwards and everyone was singing and cheering. Never did I ever think I would end up working for MFC.

BORO 0 – 0 SWINDON TOWN
AYRESOME PARK, TUESDAY SEPTEMBER 16TH 1969
GARY BOLTON

My dad took me to my first Boro game when I was a young lad. It was on Tuesday September 16th 1969 against Swindon Town and the match itself ended in an instantly forgettable 0-0 draw. That may explain why I do not remember the match itself! However, it was the sights, smells and sounds that I do recall.

Walking along cobbled Warwick Street and looking up at the seemingly towering gates adorned with 'MIDDLESBROUGH AFC' across the top. The smell of the liniment oil emanating from the players dressing rooms as we made our way towards our entrance in the North Stand and the smell of pipe-smoke wafting around from the old guy checking our tickets. The creaking of the wooden steps that led us up to our seats. The noise from the crowd as the players took to the pitch and for the first time witnessing so many people together in one place. Then perhaps the longest lasting memory of all… seeing the lush green Ayresome Park turf get brighter as darkness fell and the floodlights took full effect. To this day watching football under lights is still special to me.

Thirty two years after my 'debut' I took my young lad to his first ever Boro game. The match itself ended in an instantly forgettable 0-0 draw. That might explain why he does not remember the match itself! However, it was the sights, smells and sounds that he does recall…

INDEX